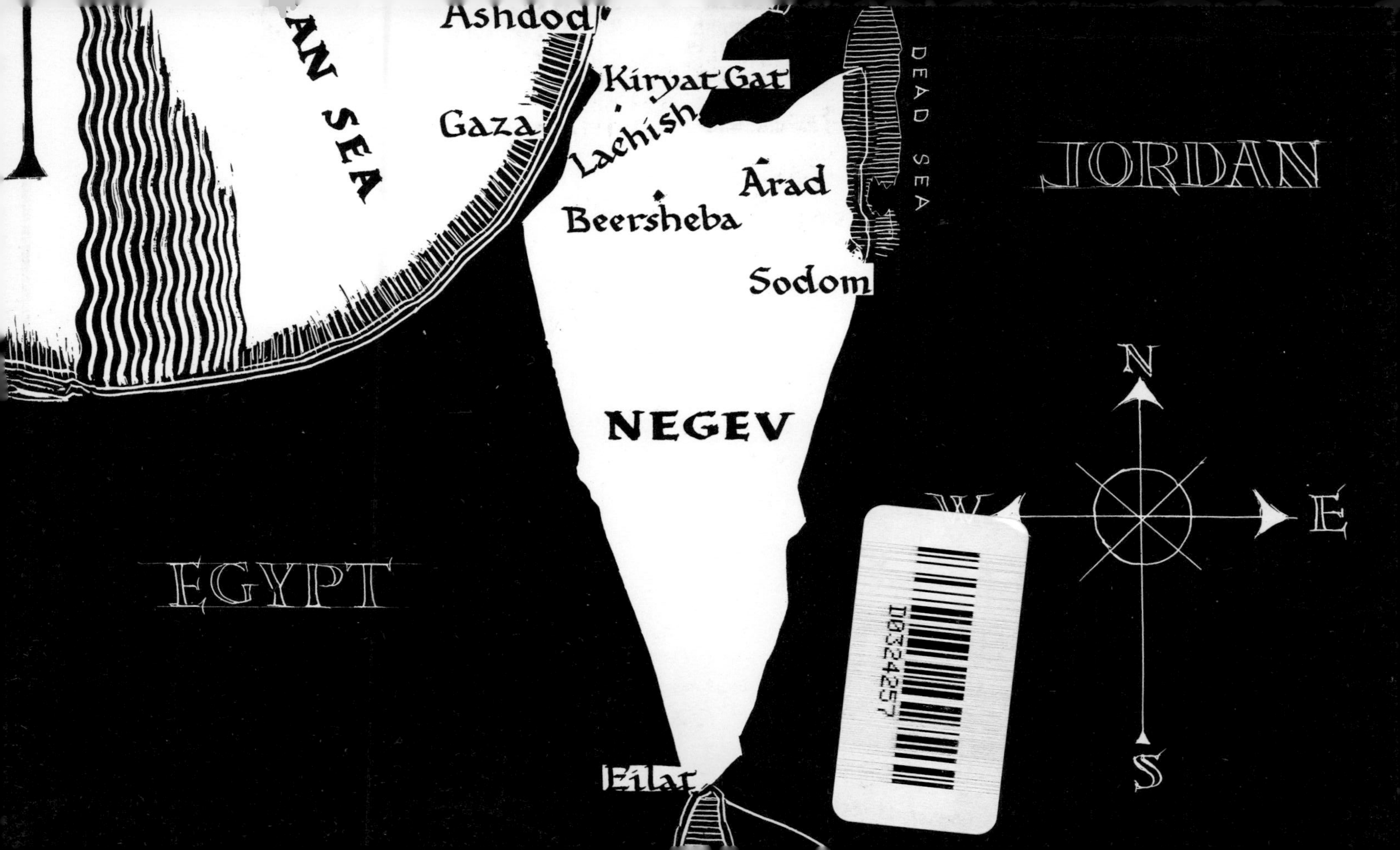

JORDAN

E

N   S

W

DEAD SEA

Sodom

Arad

Kiryat Gat

Lachish

Beersheba

Ashdod

Gaza

NEGEV

EILAT

AN SEA

EGYPT

D0324257

Israeli
Interlude

By the same author

NEW NIGERIANS
BAGHDAD AND BEYOND
A SEASON IN SARAWAK
A WORLD ELSEWHERE V. S. O.

ISRAELI
INTERLUDE

by Mora Dickson

WITH ILLUSTRATIONS
BY THE AUTHOR

RAND McNALLY & COMPANY
CHICAGO · NEW YORK · SAN FRANCISCO

for
Gershon and Ruth,
who made this visit possible

Library of Congress Catalog Card Number: 66-15010

Rand McNally & Company edition, published in the United States and possessions in 1966

Contents

JERUSALEM:
STORM OVER
DAVID'S TOWER

Prologue

'You must write a book,' they said.

'Oh no,' I replied. 'I'm not going to be corrupted that way. I don't believe in people writing books after short visits.'

'I don't know what you mean,' they said. 'It's the short-term visitor who sees most acutely because everything is new and fresh.'

'Now that's a clever rationalisation,' I thought. 'But I don't get caught that way.'

. . . . .

'I'll do a lot of drawings, though,' I thought. 'I can do them for fun. And if I did make a picture book, that is quite legitimate.'

. . . . .

'I've done a lot of drawings,' I thought. 'But they don't seem to make a book by themselves and it's a pity not to use them.'

So I have written a book after all.

JAFFA FROM TEL AVIV

CHAPTER I

Background to a Visit

PASSING the National Gallery in London one day a week or so before we left for Israel I had gone in to look at the Rembrandts. They surveyed me out of their frames, those superb portraits of real men and women who had lived and loved and suffered, depicted not only with a masterly cunning of hand but also with a profound human sympathy and understanding. Among them was a portrait of a Jewish rabbi. A middle-aged man in a flat black velvet cap and with a full dark beard, he gazed introspectively out of the picture at his own life with its overtones of persecution and tragedy. The straining unfocussed eyes held a sense of loss, a look of searching for something unlikely to be found. I stood in front of him for a long time, almost able to believe that he might rouse himself out of his reverie and speak to me. He personified one image of the Jew which was in my mind and I wondered what he would have said if I could have told him that I was about to set foot in the Promised Land, after all these centuries the State of Israel. Seldom had a new country, fought for, worked for, been born so weighted with history and hope.

At about the same time we met a young Israeli woman who told us something of her own family history, and this too became part of the mosaic which coloured our preconceived ideas.

'My great-grandfather,' she said, 'came from Morocco. In his own country he was a patriarch, a man of standing with sons and grandsons, flocks and herds and possessions. He was old, but he still had one great ambition. He desired passionately to die in Jerusalem. At least to see the Promised Land before he died.

'One day he knew that if he were to fulfil this wish then he must act soon or it would be too late. So he gathered together his sons and his sons' sons, and their wives and children, and all the relatives who formed his household, and he told them that he was re- solved to go to Jerusalem. There was no dissent. It was his wish and he was the patriarch, but they recognised too that this desire was both valid and important.

'They began to convert their possessions into cash so that they might buy a boat. They were not seafarers by trade or inclination, and perhaps none of them had any real idea what it was that they were undertaking, nevertheless they did find a vessel, and bought her, and the men set about preparing it for the voyage. It was not unlike another Noah preparing, under God's direction, the ark. Then one day the ship was ready, and the old man and all his prop- erty, along with the sons and the daughters and their house- holds and possessions embarked on her and set sail along the Mediterranean for Asia Minor.

'There is no knowing what the hardships were or how long it took those landsmen to master the arts of the sea. But they travelled in faith, and faith eventually brought them one evening out of the setting sun to where, on the long flat coastline, lay the port of Jaffa. Now Jaffa had no natural harbour, it has not to this day, and nor has Tel Aviv its new, overwhelming neighbour. The land was too flat and straight for that. And so, in the dying light, the ship lay off-shore until the next morning it could approach closer to discharge its cargo. I have no doubt that the old man couched on the deck and feasted his eyes on the land he had come so far to see, and that he thanked God for the mercy of being allowed to complete this voyage.

'But Jaffa has another characteristic, which it still retains. It is subject to sudden, sharp and very fierce storms. During that night such a tempest rose with abrupt fury. It may be that on the ship they had relaxed their guard knowing the end to be in sight, feeling the dangers to be in the past; perhaps, in preparation for the morrow, they had piled their possessions upon the deck. No one knows. But in the maelstrom the ship overturned and every soul on board was lost. Or nearly every soul. In the morning, washed up on the beach, there was found the only survivor, a thirteen-year-old boy.

'That was my great-grandfather,' she said.

But the story did not end there. The boy was taken in by friendly people and cared for. He proved not only intelligent and able, but also determined by hard work to make his mark on this new country which he had entered in such tragic fashion. Perhaps he felt too that in him lay the only fulfilment of all the hopes and dreams which had braved the terrors of that journey from Morocco. At any rate he worked hard and gradually he began to build for himself, first a business, then a reputation, then considerable wealth. Now there is a whole quarter in Tel Aviv which bears witness to his industry and his stubborn will not only to survive but to create.

This background, which seemed so dramatic when related to us in Europe, we were later to feel was not so extraordinary when viewed from the soil of Israel.

Then there was Pamela. She was dark, pretty, with a fair tender skin. Pamela had just been on her very first visit to Israel, an experience full of emotional and idealistic appeal for a young British Jew. She described all that she had seen and done in glowing terms, culminating in the final accolade.

'Do you know,' she said: 'all my life I've suffered dreadfully from the sun. I can't go out in it without protection. But in Israel I lay on the beach at Tel Aviv for hours and I never burnt at all.'

For her, in Israel, the sun stood still. And this too was an attitude that we were to encounter later.

CHAPTER II

The Day we went to Israel by way of Budapest

PEASANT WOMAN

IT WAS pre-dawn, six o'clock on a pouring wet November morning, when we left our home to go to Israel. The streets were empty and the orange lighting was reflected brokenly in the pools along the pavement. It seemed a morning to be lying snugly in bed rather than starting off on a journey to a new and unknown country.

To visit what was also practically an unknown friend, seen twice and after that taken on trust.

Some months before, in the relaxed atmosphere of high summer, my husband had gone to a conference in the Netherlands. It was to bring together in a remote Dutch country hotel a number of experienced men from different countries. On arrival in Amsterdam he was informed that a car awaited him and that another delegate was already ensconced in it. He hurried out to the entrance and, with some small fuss about luggage, settled himself beside this man.

As the car drew away on its two hours' journey they began to talk and it soon became obvious that they had much in common. The delegate in question came from Israel: his work was in the Foreign Training Department of the Israeli Ministry of Agriculture. He was concerned with the training of young men from Kenya, Tanzania, Jamaica, and other countries of the developing world, in improved agricultural techniques, particularly where these were combined with an attitude of mind that had regard to the whole of community

14

living. My husband, though lacking any agricultural expertise, had worked overseas in the field of community development and they were soon deep in conversation. After some time they began to draw upon personal anecdote and incident to illustrate a thesis, and more and more they discovered parallels in their ways of thinking and the conclusions to which experience had brought them.

The stranger began to relate how he had fought with the underground and the lessons that this had taught him. Greatly interested my husband considered in his own mind what nationality this man had been before he became a new Israeli. Was it Polish, the name sounded possible? Or had he been a Czech, or one of the other eastern European states? At any rate the enemy had been a common one, and much of what he said was fascinating.

As they neared the hotel a phrase struck odd upon my husband's ear. Had he heard aright? It was repeated, and suddenly all that had been discussed took on a different complexion altogether. It had not been a European underground at all: the enemy was not Germany as he had supposed; the enemy was Britain, the underground in Palestine, and all the activities that he had heard retold with such enjoyment had been directed against his own people, the British. It was a curious sensation. A sudden swift view, for an instant in time until the perspective readjusted itself again, of ourselves as others see us.

This was Gershon, who invited us to Israel and who, when we took him at his word, became a real friend.

In torrential rain at London Airport, with a weak, watery dawn struggling up out of the eastern sky, it seemed a flimsy enough acquaintanceship on which to have hung a month's holiday on the shores of the Mediterranean.

We were going via Budapest. Here too we were to see friends who were completely unknown, but with whom we had a tie stretching back over seven years. We were going to visit the parents of a young man who in the winter of 1956–57 had come over the Austro–Hungarian frontier as a refugee.

It so happened that at that time, and at the particular point on the frontier – Andau near the Neusiedlersee – at which a group of young men had chosen to make a crossing, my husband and I were manning a mobile canteen for the World Council of Churches. It was the most frightening experience of my life, and in some ways one of the most frustrating.

We were on leave that autumn from work overseas and one December morning a telephone call to our home in Edinburgh had asked my husband if he spoke German, if he had an international driving licence and if he were free for some time. On getting an answer in the affirmative the voice on the other end of the wire asked if he would take a mobile canteen for the World Council of Churches to the Austro–Hungarian frontier. He said 'Yes' at once, and then came to tell me that we were going. It had to be us — for how else could the canteen be operated? Alone I would certainly have hesitated. I might even have refused: this way there was no alternative except to agree.

We drove the canteen from Edinburgh, where it had originally been fitted out to bring cheer to troops in Cyprus — a fact which later proved it to be thoroughly unsuitable for work in subzero European temperatures — right across Europe to Vienna. We hurried down the autobahns of Germany, taking turns in driving, spurred on by a sense of urgency and need. We drove into Vienna late one evening, tired, dirty, certain of our welcome, only to find that no one really expected us, there was no accommodation arranged and our usefulness seemed problematical. It was a moment typical of the whole experience of the next three months, varying between times of high drama and the satisfaction of a need fulfilled and long, slow frustrating hours filled only with a bitter elusive sense of unreality.

To begin with, to our surprise, it was hard to find a place where we could operate at all. We lived during the first week or two in the small provincial capital of Eisenstadt, and every night about eight o'clock we took out the canteen and drove hopefully round the flat, forbidding countryside, on long roads often wreathed in fog, looking for a place where someone needed our help. Here, where a triangle of Austria protruded into Hungary, there were many miles of common frontier. The dark earth with its covering of crisp snow stretched out towards a limitless horizon, confusing refugees and rescuers alike as to where the line of demarcation actually ran. Surely in all this waste of space there would be opportunity for us. But it appeared not. Certain crossing places were marked and known, and here there was always a group of helpers, from famous international agencies or from small voluntary organisations, established and operational and resenting our intrusion. Competition was fierce along the frontier, and there were moments in the frozen

darkness when rival groups met beside a huddle of frightened and bewildered escapees and, in a dozen different languages but with a tone which was universal, a voice said: 'Excuse me. My refugees I think.'

We had begun to feel that we were there for decoration only, a kind of flag of propaganda as we drove about, when one night, more in despair than with any real hope of success, we turned down a rutted farm track through desolate frozen fields to a canal which formed the frontier at this point. A rumour had reached us that down there, away off the normal roads and more obvious village frontier posts, a group of students operated as couriers to little bands of people who arrived, despairing, on the other bank of the canal.

We bumped and lurched down the raised embankment of the track telling each other that this was our last attempt; if this failed we would pack up and return home. It was nearing Christmas, but only the sparkling stars provided a common factor with the Christmases we had usually known. We seemed to be the last people in the world driving an enormous white elephant of a vehicle off the rim of time. We doused the lights as we approached the dividing canal, and as the shape of a forbidding wooden watchtower gradually

17

grew out of the darkness on the other side our hearts began to beat unpleasantly fast. It was cold, and dark, and silent, and deserted.

Or so it appeared. Suddenly, out of the night, an Austrian sentry box loomed up and inside it two figures huddled in an attempt to keep warm. When they saw us they came out, amazed. They were two of the student group, composed of all nationalities from the universities of the West, who had chosen to work in this remote spot because they alone possessed the stamina and the enterprise to do so. When they saw us, and recognised our purpose, there was no doubt of their welcome. From then on we became the focus of their work, driving out each night in the freezing darkness, down the narrow track, always approaching the end with the same queezy feeling of uncertainty, to stay till dawn, feeding, resting and consoling not only those who came across but also those who made it possible for them to do so.

Here, at this point, the canal presented a formidable barrier. It ran in a straight line for some miles on either side of us, but directly opposite a road led out of Hungary which connected far back with a railway line and tempted many groups of refugees to try to escape this way. When they came to the canal bank and realised that there was no bridge it was too late. Either they must return a long way into the interior to make a detour, or be caught by the regular patrols which passed along the bank from watchtower to watchtower. Or they must cross. But how? In freezing weather: groups with women and children, many of them already exhausted by the long walk. And ironically, by some freak of its composition, the canal never froze so there was no help that way.

This problem was solved, simply, straightforwardly and without fuss, by a young Norwegian and an American student studying in Paris. They went into Vienna, visited a sports shop and bought with their own money a collapsable rubber boat. This they transported back on a bus, hid in the reeds by day, inflated as darkness fell and used as a life raft, literally a life raft, by night. Only young men could have done this, because it needed not only courage but a kind of direct simplicity, uncluttered by qualifications or consequences, which is the prerogative of the young. This was what was required, they asked no permission and they did it.

When we had found this place, and established that here we could do a job which was both needed and useful, we looked for accommodation in the nearest village of Andau at the end of the track. This

was not easy. Eastern Austria does not at all resemble its western sister, the much publicised holiday ground, full of lovely mountains, good hotels, and hot chocolate drunk on terraces in dazzling sunshine. Andau, small, desperately poor, set in flat, mist-laden country, was already as full as it could be with representatives from all the welfare associations of Europe. In the one hotel the beds were full double shift; those who worked at night falling thankfully in the morning into the sheets of those who worked by day. At last, through the good offices of the priest, we found a widow who had a spare room which she was willing to rent us. The room was freezing cold, although with a wood-burning stove in one corner. This we had to keep going ourselves, and as we worked at night and slept most of the day there was rarely the time to light and stoke the fire. We came in in the early morning, stiff and tired, our clothes rigid on us, filthy from wrestling with a vehicle which was totally unprepared to face such conditions, and fell into the huge bed under a mountainous duvet. At 3 p.m., when already it was beginning to grow dark again, we crawled out, bone-sore and exhausted, and, as best we could washed ourselves and the interior of our vehicle in scanty cold water. There was little food in Andau, and what there was was strictly portioned out on priorities. At last, after some days of near starvation on chocolate and apples kindly donated us by the Swiss, the German Red Cross offered to give us one meal a day, at seven o'clock in the evening before we left again for our night's work.

CROSSING THE BORDER

This consisted, normally, of a wonderful bowl of hot soup with vegetables or cereals in it, and on red letter days we also had meat.

This then was our way of life when we drove out one night in early February to what was by now an accustomed routine. The vehicle was turned, with considerable difficulty, at the end of the track, so that in an emergency we faced back in the right direction. I insisted on this precaution, not fancying a confrontation with the Hungarian frontier guards without a prepared escape route. We would open up the canteen, get ready the urn of hot tea, into which a good dollop of rum was put, and sit down to wait for customers. Inside the van it was warm and snug above the waist where the heat from the Calor gas stove circulated, below the waist the air froze along the floor. Outside in the darkness there was an eerie silence heavy with menace which seemed to emanate from the brooding, evil watchtower. The students stood about listening for the sounds which would tell them that there were people abroad, or walked along the line of the canal, testing the crispness of the snow and timing the passing of the communist patrols. Every now and then a hare would thump in its form, causing hearts to stop with momentary terror, or we would be paralysed by the swish and flare of a Verey light, sent up from the opposite bank to illumine our doings and warn us that we were observed. The ghastly, lurid glow cast by these rockets added another dimension to what was already a nightmare.

By now, so late in the season, the nature of the refugee groups that were arriving had changed. At first they had been family parties, a cross section of the whole Hungarian nation, or groups of workers from the same trade who had together decided to make a bid for the West. Then there began to come groups of Jews. They were fleeing not so much from present persecution as from the fear of future pogrom. Rebellions such as this stirred up ugly feelings, and, whoever came ultimately to power, they feared that a wave of anti-semitism would result. So they packed their most precious portable possessions and left, demanding from us on the frontier taxis to take them to relatives in Vienna while they made arrangements for their ultimate resting place. Later, as the cold struck fiercer, the age of the groups had dropped; it was no longer possible for the elderly to make the exhausting journey by foot. Now, with stricter supervision also in evidence, it was only the very young and active, the boys who felt the urgency of adventure to spur them on, who were able to cross this frontier.

21

In the early hours of one morning a group such as this, youngsters between fifteen and eighteen, arrived. They came from Budapest and much of the journey had had to be undertaken on foot because to be seen travelling on any sort of public conveyance invited investigation. One boy in this group spoke a little German, none of the others anything except Hungarian or Russian, so my husband began to talk to him.

'You must be tired,' he said, looking at the boy's young face topped by a small knitted cap.

'Tired!' was the reply, scorn in every tone of it: 'Certainly not. We are sportsmen. Wir sind sportler!'

Interested, my husband asked, 'And what is your sport?'

To which the boy replied: 'Schwimmen! Swimming!' and he opened the minute rucksack which contained all his possessions and showed, in pride of place on top, a pair of swimming trunks. It was incongruous, in the middle of the night, a few yards from a hostile frontier, in mid-winter and freezing cold, that this lad should be displaying as all-important his swimming trunks.

'Where do you want to go to now?' asked my husband, 'Which country? Britain? America? Holland? France?'

To which the boy replied passionately: 'Anywhere. Anywhere. So long as I can swim!'

Interested and amused we gave him our address, so that at least he could feel that he knew one family in the strange world to which he had come. Some weeks later we had a letter from Holland, where he had gone, telling us that he was settled and was swimming. Months later a very guarded letter arrived from Budapest, from his father, saying: 'It has come to my ears that in a time of crisis in the life of my son you were very good to him. Please accept the thanks of a heart-broken father.'

This was how we had come to meet Stephen, with whom we had kept up ever since and whose parents we were now about to visit, seven years later, in Budapest.

During those years, each Christmas, we had exchanged greetings and sometimes a short and guarded note. We feared to compromise the Hungarian family by too close contact. In the summer of 1963, however, Stephen had told us that his parents had been allowed to come out of Hungary to visit him and to meet the Dutch daughter-in-law whom he had presented to them, so we felt that there was no longer the same need on our part for excessive circumspection.

Finding that we could route ourselves to Israel via Budapest we wrote and asked if we might be allowed to spend a night there, and received a touching and enthusiastic response.

But plans made in connection with long international journeys are perilous things, dependent on a thousand uncontrollable factors. 'Time to spare, go by air' they say, and the truth of this became obvious at Cologne airport. As the rain poured down and the forty-five minutes stop lengthened into fifty, an hour, an hour and a half and still the plane showed no signs of leaving, we saw our afternoon on the Danube slipping quietly away. Like doctors with patients who were too temperamental to be told the truth, the cabin staff hovered around us consoling us with polite murmurs and promises of a start very shortly. Reluctantly, at last, they gave us lunch, and a rumour whose source remained unknown went round that the aircraft had broken down and a message had gone back to Brussels to send another. This caused the passengers, hitherto a conglomeration of differing nationalities, ages and outlooks, to cohere into a unity banded against all airline officials from the lavatory attendants to the aloof, supercilious pilots. It would not have taken much provocation for open hostilities to break out. We retain still an ancient crowd mentality, in situations where our interests are affected even as superficially as this, which is little altered by the liberal tolerance of the times.

Sitting in a row by themsleves, with us though not of us, were a group of elderly women, peasant women by the look of them with work-worn hands, clad all in black with white head-scarves. They accepted the delay with patience and an air of inevitability. They seemed incongruous among the rest of us and we wondered, but could not discover, what purpose had taken them on an international airline away from the homes to which they were now, presumably, returning.

At four o'clock the British, my husband and myself, created a mild sensation by asking for tea. This flung both staff and passengers into confusion. Neither Cologne airport nor a Belgian airline scheduled tea as an obligatory meal, and they saw no reason to accept responsibility for it. We argued that we should have been in Budapest by this time, it was not our fault that we were not. Tea was a standard meal with us and the airline agreed to provide passengers with standard meals during a flight.

Sides were realigned while this argument went on. Some of the

Europeans obviously felt that, after all, they were more akin to the Belgian stewardess than to the peculiar British, and there was a good deal of sibilant muttering around us. The stewardess, however, gave in, and the whispering changed to expressions of envy as we, alone of all the throng, were brought lemon tea in long glasses. It just showed that it did not pay to abandon a party allegiance and desert to the enemy!

At long last, when we had almost given up hope and were devastated by the recognition of what this delay must have done to the plans of our Hungarian friends, it was announced that a fresh plane had arrived and we were on our way.

It was dark when we touched down at Budapest. What should have been an arrival in the early afternoon with pale winter sunshine to greet us now became a furtive scurrying into the echoing Customs Hall of a half-shut-down airport with no one, apparently, quite knowing who we were or what we should do. Language was not easy, although my husband's good German was a considerable help.

Anxious and agitated we eyed the trolleys that came in with luggage, our nervousness increasing as each one discharged its load and still our suitcases had not appeared. At last it became obvious that there was no more to come, and we were baggageless. On top of everything else this seemed to be a major disaster, only mitigated when we discovered that several of our fellow passengers were in the same situation. They, however, were staying in Budapest with time to institute enquiries, while we flew on to Israel early next morning.

In the meantime I had investigated, round a shabby screen, up a passage and past a formidable female official to see if I could discover Stephen's family. It seemed all too likely that they might also by this time have disappeared. However when my face came round the jamb of a half-open door I saw a move in my direction. Two men came towards me, one young with smooth dark hair, a charming smile and, praise be, a little English: the other small, thin, desperately harassed, clutching in his hands a bouquet of roses which six hours before had been fresh and dewy but now hung in a limp, bedraggled bunch. This was Stephen's younger brother and his father. During all this delay they had remained at the airport, phoning back at intervals to the mother at home in their flat altering meals, cancelling a car which had been arranged to take us on a

24

trip by the Danube, putting off visitors who were to come and greet us, gradually being reduced, in their capacity as hosts, to a state of nervous apoplexy.

I accepted the roses and went back to my husband. We decided, there and then, that whatever happened to the luggage, whether we saw it again or arrived in Israel for a month with an overnight bag, we must now forget it entirely and concentrate on making what remained of the visit enjoyable both for ourselves and our hosts. It appeared that the luggage had, in any case, gone on to Bucharest, so we could only leave our name and an address and hope for the best.

This was the nadir: after this the visit began to recover. We went through passport control determined to let nothing stop us enjoying ourselves. But it was obvious that although we felt like that the Doctor was far from achieving the same optimism. By this time the airport bus into the city had gone, and as taxis had to be ordered out specially and the time had long gone by for this, our hosts were faced with the embarrassing situation of having to propose that we go by public transport on an ordinary autobus. Embarrassing for them perhaps, for us, as we did our best to reassure them, this was an added interest to the trip. Far from regretting the segregation of the private conveyance we welcomed the chance to see something, however fleeting, of the ordinary life of average people. So we climbed into the autobus and rattled off the long distance into Budapest, a journey which necessitated changing vehicles at a junction just inside the city bounds.

There was the added bonus of a number of extra conversational gambits, which were welcome as it suddenly seemed quite difficult to find much in common to talk about. This strain was increased by the fact that the Doctor spoke no English at all and my husband had therefore to carry the whole burden of the conversation with him in German, while I soon discovered that the young brother was not quite so fluent in my language as I had supposed.

We sat on wooden seats and bumped cheerfully along, peering out to see what we could see. It was an unfair first glimpse of a city which has been famed for its beauty. Enormous buildings soared up into gloom above inadequate street lighting. Huge broad streets, made it seemed for festivals and displays, for triumphal marches of exuberant crowds, stretched away into ghostly darkness, dwarfing the isolated figures glimpsed at bus stops or in the occasional flare of a shop window. I wondered how far I was seeing what I had expected to see, and remembered the effect on a stranger of entering London through the approaches to Liverpool Street Station.

Inside the bus, however, all was cheerfulness and friendliness. Only one small incident marred this impression. As we got up to leave at the stop where we were changing buses my husband was rudely and deliberately jostled by a man standing close to him. He was disconcerted by this, there being no apparent reason for such an action, then he caught a half-understood phrase which seemed to explain it. He had been speaking in German, and it was towards his supposed nationality that hostility was felt.

At last we alighted in the centre of the town and began to walk the final few yards to what had been our destination since six that morning. Over us colossal buildings towered, not the fragile glass structures of the twentieth century but great stone palaces, or so it seemed, heavy with architrave and balustrade, solid with the dignity of the passing of ancient regimes and the withstanding of modern revolutions. We entered through a great wooden door, inside which the concierge sat in a little wooden box eyeing the inhabitants of her domain and noting their goings out and their comings in. An admirable system, as it had proved itself to be, in times past when concern with one's neighbour's doings had been perverted from a virtue into a vice.

Inside, the building struck colder still. It was constructed four-square round a huge courtyard. The great stone balconies reared up towards the stars. Our footsteps echoed on the empty stairs. It was easy to imagine such a place tainted by the agonies of those who had found themselves caught up in terror with no way out and had flung themselves, despairing, on to the paving far below. By the time we arrived we were not only out of breath, we were also haunted by our own chimera.

Once inside the flat, however, although the rooms remained cavernous, all height like gigantic halls distorted by subdivision out of their true proportions, the atmosphere of warmth and friendliness which greeted us speedily dispelled our apprehensions. Stephen's mother, much younger than I had anticipated and wholly charming, may have suffered housewifely crises over the wrecking of her culinary plans but she let none of this appear. Her concern was all for our discomforts and in one respect she greatly set our minds at rest. Behind her an elderly gentleman of very distinguished appearance leant forward to be introduced. This was a professor who had instructed the Doctor in his youth and then, a generation later, his sons and who had now been included in the party to greet us because he spoke admirable English. We gathered that there had been other guests but these had been sent home when it became obvious that we were going to arrive so very late. For this, while regretting the upheaval on our hosts' side, we were profoundly grateful. For all our determination to think of nothing but enjoyment the strain of events was beginning to take its toll.

The visit really began when we sat round a table covered with a dark chenille cloth in the inner communicating sitting-room and drank a glass of cognac together to celebrate our meeting.

They were middle-class professional people living shabbily and quietly, not afraid exactly, still enormously proud of their city and their people, but treading delicately, waiting and watching. It was a grief to them to have Stephen separated from them by barriers of ideology as well as distance; perhaps it was also some embarrassment. It was never clear why he had gone across the border when he did and it certainly did not seem that it had been a matter of vital political urgency. I got the same impression that we had so often had during those long nights in the cold on the frontier, that many of the young went as much from a sense of adventure and curiosity as from any real conviction or need. In 1956, for the first time for many years, due to a political policy of coexistence, the frontier to the west was open, free of its barriers, its barbed wire and its mines. When the news of this percolated back to the interior a rising tide of excitement made many whose lives were, in spite of everything, tolerable nevertheless feel that they must take this chance, must find out for themselves if 'freedom' was all they dreamed it was. So curiosity, genuine desire, adventure, a deep Magyar instinct for migration, necessity and even a kind of keeping up with the Joneses, all played their part in bringing those thousands over the border: and for many, who did not fully recognise the irrevocableness of the step which they were taking, it ended in being a bitter decision once the drama and the headlines had passed on.

The West was not without blame in this situation, and it should have shown us, had we been humble enough to read the lessons aright, what was wrong with our own society rather than what we condemned in other people's. For we encouraged this exodus, as we had to some extent encouraged the holocaust which preceded

27

it. We held out promises, without any deep thought about the reality of their fulfilment in every day terms. We bandied about words like 'freedom' and 'choice' and 'Christian love' and when faced with a people accepting us at our own valuation we failed miserably. For we did not love them, not as many of them had been loved at home: there was precious little freedom, in the most basic sense, for the young man or woman who ended up in a camp in Austria or later in a mining hostel in Britain, and what there was was freedom to feel lonely, and homesick, and an object of faint derision. We were the golden West, but we wanted our gold for ourselves when it came down to it. We had not recognised that in a changing world it was now going to be how we behaved at home that was more important than what we said abroad. Young men like Stephen, who survived the experience and eventually settled in to their new countries, had needed to call upon all their resources of courage and stubbornness and individual pride to do so.

The professor, with old world courtesy combined with a genuine eagerness, had seated himself beside me to talk. He wanted to talk English again and as the polished, correct phrases flowed from him I asked when he had last visited Britain.

'I have only been once,' he replied gently, 'and that was in 1910. But I remember it all very clearly.'

It then transpired that in 1910 he had gone as a delegate to a great World Missionary Conference in Liverpool and the names and faces of all those whom he had met at that time were fresh and vivid to him still. He hoped that they would be as vivid to me; carried away by his enthusiasm he failed to realise that I had not even been born when he was making his only visit to my country. But I did not altogether fail him. By a curious chance my father had also taken a vital interest in this same conference and in what stemmed from it, and so I did remember some of the names, long since forgotten, which still with him reverberated with greatness. For a short space his past was also my past, and though what we remembered had totally different connotations for each of us there was sufficient common ground to give us both pleasure.

The mother had prepared a meal for us. Goodness knows whether it was only the last of many to be made ready and then discarded. She did not reveal. We sat round the table and ate open sandwiches laden with a variety of sweet and savoury things, and while we did so we related to them at first hand our meeting with their son in the

28

cold and fear and darkness of a frontier seven years before. They wept. We wondered afterwards if we had done right to present them vividly again with the choices and emotions of that time. I think we did, if only because we gave the mother one more piece to fit into the picture she cherished of her son.

No sooner had we finished eating, it seemed, than after some whispering the professor put a proposition to us. Although it was already late they would like to take us out to a restaurant, to give us some idea of the city. They had arranged a drive in the afternoon, but that had had to be cancelled, now all that remained possible was to entertain us in this way.

We were appalled. By now exhausted, having survived a day of sixteen hours and fraught with difficulties and delays, we longed only to go quietly to bed. I looked at my husband, and he looked back despairingly at me. I started to say that we really wanted only to talk to them and then to rest, and I stopped. We looked at each other again. It was impossible. We had already ruined all their plans, they wished to do us honour and we had no right to refuse them this.

'Thank you,' we said, 'We would like to come, but please do not expect us to eat a large meal because the journey has upset us a little.'

So we put on our outdoor clothes again and sallied forth into the night.

The air revived us, and the method of transport roused our interest and curiosity. We went by the Budapest underground, something which we had not even known to exist. Those who live in London are apt to assume that their underground railway system is unique. True they have heard of the underground in Moscow, they know of the Metro in Paris and will occasionally concede that in its method of signposting and its concern for pregnant women and war wounded it has a slight moral superiority, but to find that other cities too have thought of solving some of their traffic problems this way comes often as a shock.

The Budapest underground was a railway in the real sense of the word. It was reached by a very shallow staircase, which gave the feeling that it was not genuinely underground at all and must surely be shaking the paving stones above as it steamed along.

I cannot swear to it, but my impression as the train came in was of an old-fashioned, long-funnelled steam engine, drawing a series of elegant, upright wooden coaches. Certainly the whole had an air of a time of greater leisure and spaciousness and of imperial days. Ladies in lavish dresses could have swept into these carriages with ease, the train proceeded at a stately pace and even the stations seemed wider and more human than the long narrow tunnels through which our trains burst. I dare say that in the press and hurry of the daytime rush the impression given would have been quite otherwise, but in the easy emptiness of late evening it seemed, somehow, a gracious way to travel.

When we climbed into the upper world again, to hurry through streets nearly empty of people or of traffic, we were restored in humour and even looking forward to the entertainment.

The buildings continued enormous, massive against the stars, with every now and then a gap where construction work was going on and we were told that this was still the result of the war. I could not understand at first what it was about these sites that seemed so strange and made me feel so foreign. Some feature of them was familiar, and yet in the fashion of a dream, not quite remembered, tugging at the memory, accepted and rejected all in one. And then I knew. The scaffolding which buttressed the walls was made of wood. A forest grew across the pavement of thick tree trunks intricately patterned to support the working platforms. Suddenly it was extraordinary to recognise that this was something I had once taken for granted as an ordinary daily sight in my own life, and that without my noticing or realising change it had long ago been super-ceded by the spidery lace of slim metal poles. Time seemed to con-certina, my fixed pattern of the world dissolved, those sturdy wooden beams reminded me that not everybody thought as we did, grew in the way that we had grown, accepted our glib modernity.

We came at last to a street near the river, the Danube whose very name is evocative of a world of romance. Near at hand the gi-gantic structure of a new, or renewed, bridge, in the background the round dark hills of Pest showed black against a navy sky. Beneath them we were very small. It was only when we climbed up on to a wooden catwalk and entered a door in a wall, within which there was light and music and a passage leading down into a painted cellar, that proportion was again restored and we found ourselves human among other humans.

The cellar itself was full of a lively and noisy company, though not really gay. A little band of rather fat and elderly gentlemen

30

played wild gypsy music on violins and the harsh full glare of the electric light made no concession to sophistication or sentiment. But what was lacking in the *mise-en-scène* was amply counterbalanced by our hosts, and by the food. Delicately sensitive to our lightest whim the former calculated to a nicety our appetite for the latter. The result was that freed from the fear both of excessive gluttony and of being an expensive luxury to our friends, we could enjoy to the full the delicious Hungarian fish dish that was set before us, and even the struggle with communication took a turn for the better when much of what was said was, in any case, drowned by the wailing rhythm of a fiddle in one's ear.

At midnight honour on all sides was amply satisfied and we emerged from our pseudo-cellar into the upper air. Here, however, a snag developed. All transport had stopped. Our little train had finally retired underground for the night and closed its iron gates upon us. The streets were silent and deserted: only the bridge and Pest still soared darkly towards the sky. There seemed just one solution and throwing discretion and financial stringency to the winds the Doctor led us to two taxis lurking forlornly in a rank and we were driven home in state.

I had been somewhat exercised since we arrived about where we slept. We seemed to have seen the entire flat and I could not find an extra bedroom into which we could be fitted. When we arrived back, however, this mystery was solved. The double doors between the two reception rooms were drawn together and the inner one was quickly and expeditiously converted into a sleeping apartment. Couches were pulled apart and reconstituted as beds, our pitifully small bags were brought and we were wished a very good night. A good night—but there was not much of it left. The plane departed early the next morning and in order to get the airport bus shortly after seven we must be up and on the go by half-past five. It was a shock for our hosts to realise this; they had somehow hoped that our definition of early meant sometime in the morning which would leave the opportunity for sight-seeing and more talk. But plans were made and bookings taken and we could not change them now. Perhaps it was as well. Maybe more time would have demanded from us a different kind of relationship.

Very early next morning, dazed and exhausted, we climbed out of bed and dressed. Over our cups of tea a touching little ceremony took place when we were each presented with a beautiful picture book as a momento—one of Budapest, the city which we had never seen, and one of Hungary. Then we were taken to the bus and sent on our way.

Or at least so we thought. In fact when we reached the airport there still lay ahead of us another long, long wait. Although our plane was starting from Budapest, for reasons which we never knew it was delayed. While we sat segregated from our fellow men in the long impersonal lounge, regretting all the sleep that we might so easily have had and gazing half-heartedly through the huge plate glass windows, I saw suddenly three familiar figures approaching us across the tarmac. Chatting and laughing to each other were the Belgian hostess and her fellow stewards from off our conveyance of the day before. It was a moment or two before I recognised what this could mean: then I said to my husband:

'Quick. Go and ask them if they've still got our luggage with them. They've been to Bucharest and are now on their way back home, with any luck they'll have our cases in the plane.'

He did just that. They had. They did not seem the least surprised to see us there, or think it strange that they should have taken our baggage for the night to Bucharest. They nodded and smiled, said we could have it and passed on to their coffee and their gossip in the quarters reserved for those who live professionally in the air. We sought out the first Hungarian stewardess we could see and asked her to have our cases transferred to our onward plane which had just arrived. My husband, being wary in these matters, felt that he should check with her some ten minutes later as to whether the job had been well and truly done.

'Oh yes,' she said. 'I've labelled them for Cairo and seen that they were put aboard.'

For Cairo! In all the world perhaps the one city from which we, bound for Tel Aviv, would never have been able to recover our possessions.

It seemed then as though we might be fated. Perhaps this journey was to be a series of small mishaps, of meetings which did not quite connect and experiences which just failed to be significant. But when we circled the airport at Tel Aviv and came slowly down into a blood red sunset against which rose the black spears of cypress trees, and saw the smiling face of Gershon in the crowd, and found our baggage after all correctly readdressed, we flung off uneasy intimations of bad luck and prepared to have a splendid busman's holiday.

TEL AVIV FROM JAFFA

CHAPTER III

A Land of People

ORIENTAL GIRL

ISRAEL is full of surprises, for the Gentile as well as for the Jew, when he first sets out to see it for himself. But the most astonishing aspect of the land is its people. Gershon was the only Israeli I ever heard who used regularly to call his fellow countrymen the 'Israelites', a name which struck curiously upon our ears evoking, as it did, an ancient biblical picture of bearded, nomadic, militant tribes. No doubt we all have our own ideas of a Jewish prototype, as we have of other races; the surprise is often how nearly the reality actually does approximate to the mental image, but in Israel no preconception can survive the first encounter, so diverse is the range and so wide the coverage of her population.

Presently, in another generation or so, the Israelis will be Israelis, and the background pattern of their heritage will be history. But now, here, history is still alive and a major portion of all but the young of the population, whether they like it or not, carry with them the imprint of two secular nationalities, though their spiritual heritage they have in common. Here and now it is possible to watch the fascinating spectacle of a people who have come together from all the ends of the earth, bringing with them the customs and traditions and cultures of widely separated places, forging themselves into a nation which is, in a sense, attempting to bridge a gulf of centuries. In this tiny laboratory of humanity many of the problems are in fact still the problems of the human race, and not those of a chosen and distinctive people. It may be that some of the solutions will also come to have a wider validity.

Originally, when Israel was still just a compelling idea in the minds of the founding fathers, notably Theodore Herzl, an Austrian Jew, the tiny but increasing trickle of immigrants into the strip of middle-eastern sea coast came from Russian lands. It is interesting now to realise that Herzl himself, whose tomb rests in calm splendour on a Jerusalem hilltop, had once seriously considered, with the co-operation of the British Government, establishing the Jewish National Home in Uganda. How fascinating to speculate on what might have been the changed faces of both Africa and Asia Minor had this plan been carried out. But it had no chance of success because for the first generation which saw a real possibility of translating the age-old dream into reality it was not simply any land to call their own, it was the return to The Land of their fathers which they so ardently desired. The actual soil of Israel had a mystic significance, as it still has for many today. It was not simply the reuniting of a people who had been for generations dispersed; it was the reuniting of a people dispersed with the land of which they had been dispossessed.

So those who laid the foundations of modern Israel, long before it achieved statehood, were the intelligentsia from Eastern Europe, literate, cultured and passionately ideological. They began to come to Palestine after the great Russian pogroms of the 1880s, and once started, the flow, though small, was steady. They showed the way, they opened the gates. Embattled in their kibbutzim, wrestling with the land, as Jacob wrestled with the angel, to bring forth a new kind of social unity, they set their feet on the sacred soil and pointed their faces forward.

With the rise to power of Hitler in Germany in 1933 a new impetus was given to the need for a National Home for the Jews. Through the troubled years that followed, when the trickle grew into a stream and the dream was sometimes not far from being a nightmare, those that came, both young and old, often left behind them in Europe terrifying persecutions. Though the sacred ideal of the Promised Land still burned brightly, for many it was overlaid by a bitterer picture. The past was more powerful than the future; they fled from terror to the only place in all the world where it seemed that they had any right to go. They came for refuge, victims not pioneers, to seek strength from the Land rather than to impart strength to it, But when they had to fight for the land itself the flame leapt up once more, and this very battle which brought forth the State of Israel brought forth too unity and nationhood.

So Israel was born in 1948 and the shape of the future began to be discerned, built on the foundations of European culture which had been the background of so many of her people. This was a state which might yet form a bridge between conflicting worlds, with all that was best of the West set in the ancient soil of the East.

Then the unforeseen began to happen. As the spate of immigrants from the west steadied and then gradually diminished an astonishing phenomenon, which no one had believed existed, began to be made

plain. When the news spread around the world, into remote and far-off places, that Israel was now a state in her own right, that the Jews were no longer homeless, a rising tide of emigrants began to flow out from the lands of Asia and Africa. Whole villages in the Yemen, and in India, and in Morocco, and in Libya which had for many centuries accepted as natural their position as indigenous Jews, belonging yet separated, seemed suddenly, and often mysteriously, to know that at last there was one place in the world where the only qualification for full citizen-

KIBBUTZNIK

ship was the one attribute which had always cut them off from this very consummation—their Jewishness. And they rose up and came to claim their heritage. Out of the Yemen, in an uprooting known as Operation Magic Carpet, two complete villages packed up all their possessions, trekked down to Aden and were then flown to Israel. In one fell swoop they abandoned not only the country of their long adoption but a whole mediaeval way of life and had themselves transported by the most modern of methods slap into the twentieth

YEMENI GIRL

century. And, in varying degrees, this pattern was repeated again and again elsewhere. So that gradually the weight of western European culture, once so predominant in the Israeli state, began to be balanced by a flood of simple, primitive peoples from ancient tribal backgrounds whose aim was to find themselves a home, to establish their identity.

This has brought problems, not least the difficulties of welding into a true unity peoples so widely diverse not only in their cultures and customs but also in their educational standards. It has added a richness and variety to the life of the nation, but in doing so it has also changed the pattern which the early pioneers laid down. It has brought on to Israel's doorstep possibilities of class and racial distinction which she never dreamed would face her within her own borders, and it has produced some of the problems of urban society which a community that had turned its back on the cities of the West and fervently espoused a rural vocation had not thought to find before it. It is the Israeli attempt to discover answers, the struggle for solutions, which fascinates and intrigues the visitor from overseas.

37

Every adult Israeli to whom we spoke for any length of time seemed to have a past which was lurid in its details. After a while the astonishing thing was not these tales of horror and sorrow and inhumanity but the growing realisation of the triumphant resilience of the human spirit. In a sense this was contained for me in two words, each surrounded as time went on with their own evocative connotations. These words were 'Jew' and 'Israeli'. They had been one, and were now the other; the Jew was oppressed, maltreated, humble, anxious: the Israeli was unafraid, assured, brash perhaps, supremely confident. This conflict, this radical break with the past, brings with it two problems whose acknowledgement even as problems is only just beginning to take place. The first is the attitude of those who have been born in the State of Israel and known no other background to their fathers and through them to their age-old family history. The other, profounder, deeper, and requiring more than time to resolve it, is the ancient question so often asked before: is to be a Jew a nationality or a religion? Now the answer is urgent and could be far-reaching, for to be Israeli is not a religion, and what is the relationship of the State of Israel to be both with those within its borders who feel that it is still a Holy Land and, more difficult, with those without who choose to be Jews but not Israelis?

So much for the problems. What of the people who must deal with them? They come, many of them, from indomitable stock.

A middle-aged woman told us the story of her grandmother, one of the early pioneers when the land of Palestine was a malaria-infested swamp. The grandparents lived in Rumania, were in fact Rumanian, and the grandfather was a brilliant lawyer. But he had risen in his profession as far as he was able; he had been told openly, with kindly intent, 'It's a pity you are a Jew, you can never be a judge,' and sickened by this he determined to go to a land where he would be unlikely to use his particular talents, but where the ceiling set upon his career would be that of his own ability rather than an arbitrary decision based on racial discrimination.

By chance I felt able to understand something of what the background had been which had

ARMENIAN WOMAN

brought him to this decision. Our friends in Budapest were not Jews, but they too, for different reasons, and under a different sort of discrimination, were walking softly and taking care, aware that the stability of their lives was uncertainly based on the unpredictable goodwill of others.

Be that as it may, the grandparents packed up themselves and their family and travelled to the Middle East. Three weeks later the grandfather died of malaria, leaving his widow with five young children.

The grandmother refused to return to Rumania, which her friends urged her to do. She determined to stay, and set herself to earn enough to keep the family from starvation. She started a small business with some other immigrants, and her job was to travel, every six weeks or so, to Beirut on the Mediterranean coast to collect stores and goods. She must have been a woman not only of courage but of intelligence and energy. On one of these trips she was returning in the coach when she encountered a fierce storm. It became impossible to go further and, on a desolate stretch of the sandy track the coach was stopped and she settled inside it to sleep out the storm. The story did not relate what happened to the driver but it would seem she had little confidence in him or any others with her for she arranged all her bundles around her for safe-keeping. This was travel through wild country infested by men who would not hesitate to rob and murder.

A short while later she awoke. The storm had died away but she had the feeling that something else was also gone. She was alone, but her groping fingers could not detect anything missing in the baggage. She slept again. Once more the same thing happened. She started awake with a strong sensation that everything in the coach was not as it had been when she had settled herself for the night, but she could not discover what had changed. She was a brave and strong-minded woman and, when this had happened yet a third time, she set herself to stay awake and solve the mystery. She lay back feigning sleep and was presently aware that the baggage around her was shifting. Softly, almost imperceptibly, it was moving. Turning her head very carefully she suddenly saw, like some huge insect, a thin brown hand feeling delicately round one of her bundles. She leant swiftly over and grabbed it.

The owner of the hand, a Bedouin Arab, rose up blackly in the entrance to the coach. Without hesitation the grandmother said in Arabic, with no inflection except one of ordinary courtesy: 'How kind of you to come and guard me.'

Courtesy and hospitality are Arab virtues. She was immediately invited to visit him in his tent which was pitched nearby. Unhurried, showing nothing of agitation or anger, the grandmother climbed out of the coach and accompanied her thief across the sandhills. Once there she was ceremoniously ushered into the tent where the first thing that caught her eye was the rest of her baggage which had been carefully extracted from her carriage while she slept. She smiled. 'How good of you to protect my things,' she said, and seated herself on the rug beside them.

For the rest of the night, not daring to let herself be lulled into sleeping in case theft should also turn to murder, she told stories to the Bedouin and his family, keeping them enthralled and amused like some nineteenth-century Scheherazade. In the morning, taking it entirely for granted that they would help her, she repacked the baggage into the coach and, thanking them for their hospitality, drove off.

This was courage and a determination to survive; humanity overcoming the dangers of living. But it was a straightforward situation of human greed and cunning. This was an incident that could have happened to any traveller in those times, to be met with whatever resources he had within him. The story of Nahum, the perpetual exile, was of a different calibre, and it was not one of which we could have said 'That might have happened to us.' Its tragedy lay in this fact. For the whole calamitous essence of the story of Nahum lay in the fact that he was what he was, with no possibility of changing this reality even had he wished to do so. Nahum, who had once been called Fritz, was a Jew.

Nahum had left Germany in 1933, before the terrors of concentration camps and mass annihilation, and perhaps this very fact accounted for his being one of the few Israelis whom we had met who looked back rather than forward, and who still felt, however faintly, the pangs of exile. For he had thought of himself always as a German, and been proud to be so. His rejection by the country which he had considered to be his own had been bitter and complete, but it had not been accompanied by the savage physical indignities and horrors suffered by those who came out of Germany in later years and which had burnt away cleanly their earlier allegiancies. For Nahum the land of Germany held yet a strong and poignant pull; the German forests in particular, those dark, myth-haunted woods so different from the bright bare country of his second home.

In his scrapbook of photos there was one taken of a classroom in which a number of teenage schoolboys were having a lesson. It was an ordinary enough photograph, the bare room, the desks, the young faces, some handsome some plain, all in earnest concentration. Only one thing made it singular. In the centre of the picture an aisle ran down the room dividing it in two. On the one side sat the whole class, on the other one solitary boy.

'That was me,' said Nahum, pointing to him. 'Even then I was a Jew.'

At this point Mrs Nahum, who was sitting beside me, broke in to tell us how the knowledge had come to her that she was any different from the rest of her schoolfellows.

'I remember perfectly,' she said, 'even the date—a day in April 1933. Up till that moment I had never thought of myself as being anything except a German girl. I didn't know that I had any other background. I loved school. I was good at games, and popular and life was tremendous fun. Then, this morning, I went to school as usual. My best friend, with whom I had always done everything, came up to me in the playground and said: "My mother says I'm not to speak to you any more."

'I couldn't understand it. When I went home in great distress my mother tried to explain to me that I was a Jewess. Nothing was ever the same again.'

Nahum had not been long qualified and started in his chosen career of teaching when a letter arrived one morning dismissing him because he was a Jew. There were no euphemisms used, it was stated baldly, Jews were not good enough to teach young Germans. And this applied not just to one school, but to every school: it ended his whole career. But what to do? Where to go? He *was* a German, he did not just feel himself to be one, and could not lightly think of leaving.

He considered going to France, not so far and still within the European culture and tradition which he cherished. But he described how, on a visit to France with a friend, they had been jeered at in a cafe by young Frenchmen for being German. 'I couldn't win,' he said. 'In Germany I was a dirty Jew, in France a sale Boche.' So it seemed that Palestine, as it then was, held out the only hope of an uncrippled life.

PROBATION OFFICER

So he came to Palestine, to struggle as a teacher in Palestinian schools, to join the British in the Second World War and serve four years as a Royal Engineer, and then to take the skills that he had learnt and fight the British in a war of independence for Israel. Now, a man with a face eroded by hardship he worked as a probation officer; a gentle, thoughtful man who did not share the ebullient optimism of many of his fellow Israelis.

Yet he had had one curious piece of good fortune. Through the years he had retained, a sort of bitter momento, the letter announcing his original dismissal. When in the early 1960s the question of German reparations to individual Jews had arisen he had not, at first, thought much about it. Though his livelihood had been destroyed so long ago, he had not suffered as those who came later had suffered. Then one day coming across the letter he had thought to himself, 'Why not?', and had sent it to the investigating commission, more as an experiment than because he hoped to gain anything by it. To his surprise it had been accepted and he had received a handsome sum in reparations. It had, indeed, made the difference between a reasonable standard of living and some hardship; a social worker's pay in Israel is by no means princely.

With some of the money he and his wife had taken a journey, back to the village near Frankfurt from which he had originally come. At first, unrecognised, he had visited the old familiar scenes, looked on the house in which his family had lived. Then one day a man had known his face, his father's chauffeur, who had been suspected of being in with the Nazis. To his disgust this man had greeted him with fawning servility. There was shame, arrogance, guilt, embarrassment in the attitude of those who knew his origin. He spoke Hebrew always with his wife, for though they might speak German in Israel they felt a compulsion to speak only Hebrew in Germany. One day in a cafe they were asked where they came from. 'From Israel.' 'Are you coming back now?' 'What,' he said, 'To be kicked out again?' and then suddenly the brutal, arrogant reply: 'Take care they don't kick you up the backside over there.'

Perhaps the visit had one desirable outcome. It showed Nahum plainly the irrevocable nature of his separation from the land in which he had been born.

For those who came later from Europe the way had been harsher. One beautiful Sunday morning we were driven out of Tel Aviv to visit the only prison in Israel given over to young offenders, Tel Mond. Going round the carpentry shop my husband stopped to speak to the instructor, a fair-haired, blue-eyed man of middle age. He spoke no English so the conversation was in German and the story that emerged, told simply and without any intent to surprise or shock, was a heart-rending one.

The instructor was of Czechoslovakian origin and he recounted how during the first years of the war, because of his appearance, he had been able to pass himself off as a Gentile. But the time came at last when he was betrayed and he found himself in a concentration camp – Auschwitz. Everything in the camp was done by number, tattooed on the wrist, and by alphabetical order without reference to the humanity of those involved. So it happened that he performed every task, of whatever nature, with the next number to his own whose name also began with an H. But the next number was that of a six-year-old boy.

The time came one day when the whole camp was turned out for one of the dreadful inspections that periodically took place. They lined up in single file with all their possessions, the pitiful remnants that remained, to shuffle slowly past a row of officials, including the medical officer. And as they passed they were divided, right, left, left, right, into two groups. They knew, or at least our friend the instructor knew, that the group to the right was doomed to die, while those to the left might live a little longer.

In front of him the small boy was clutching all that he had left in

43

the world, a battered attaché case. As he came up to the guard he was roughly ordered to fling it aside on a heap of discarded objects. He refused, clinging with terrified intensity like a wizened little monkey to the only thing that was left him. In a flash the instructor behind him saw what his refusal was going to mean. Instantly he leant over the lad and wrenched the case out of his arms, flinging it on to the heap, and while the boy turned on his rescuer in a fury, sobbing and beating at him with skinny matchsticks of arms the guard laughed. But he was saved. They were both directed to the left and lived.

The war ended, the instructor had survived. He found his way to Israel and eventually to a job with the prison as a teacher of carpentry. One morning, among the new intake, he noticed a lad with a familiar number tattooed on his wrist, and a scene which he had never forgotten flashed vividly before his mind's eye. He went up to him and said: 'Your name is Julius H?' The lad said: 'Yes.'

'Do you not know me?'

'No.'

'Then lift up your sleeve. I think that you will find that the number on your wrist follows exactly on the one that I have here on mine.'

And so it was. For the second time they compared the numbers which for so long and in such dreadful circumstances had linked them to each other.

It went on. No one hastened to tell us these tales, or recounted them with any particular emotion; but equally they did not hesitate to respond to my husband's gentle probing questions. There was the man, from East Prussia, who had come to Palestine at the age of five from Warsaw to which city his parents had moved. The

whole family emigrated, but, compared with what was to come, those were still peaceful days, and six months before the war the parents returned on a visit to Poland. He never saw them again. 'All that we had left,' he said, 'was a pair of my mother's shoes.'

Or the man whose whole family emigrated from Latvia. But not his uncle. His uncle was an orthodox Jew of a deeply religious kind and to him the Promised Land was not just the physical country which might one day become Israel, hallowed by history, ready to

ISRAELI   be recreated by the descendents of the ancient

tribes. To him the Promised Land was something more – the Holy Land, an idealised, semi-mystical country to be attained only by the pure in heart. He felt that he could not go to a land called Israel where the ordinary day-to-day life would be as secular and sinful as was life in any country. Where pigs were bred, and men did not observe the Sabbath in all its strictness. He was caught in a dilemma between the dream and the reality, between the vision and the human nature of those who must give the vision substance. So, when the family left Latvia for a new life in a new country the uncle remained behind. He was killed later with others who had not succeeded in getting away. In a sense he died for his ideals, but there are those now living in Israel for whom this same dilemma is still a continuing reality.

But not every background held the horrors and the concentration camps of Europe though most had been made aware, in subtle and less subtle ways lacerating to the human spirit, of their separateness from the common lot. The Iraqi doctor described how he had been banished from the city to a remote village because he was a Jew, and we recognised what this must have meant in a country like Iraq where civilisation is an urban growth and village life to those of the professions unthinkable. But persecution went further. On the occasion of a bad motor accident he was called out to help with the casualties. They were being brought in from the desert track where the crash had occurred, on a lorry, wounded and dead all muddled up together in some dreadful macabre pile. He collected his instruments and hastened out to give his assistance, but no sooner had he arrived and prepared himself to clamber into the lorry and sort out those who still needed his aid from those who were already dead, than one of the villagers put up the cry that he was a Jew. At that the atmosphere grew hostile. 'You must not touch the dead,' they said, 'Because you are a Jew. You are a Jew. You are a Jew.' And for a Moslem it would be a defilement of the dead to be handled by a Jew. But not of the living. If he could reach them. But he could not. He must, to find out who still lived and who was already gone, touch every body in that dreadful huddle, and argue as he might the villagers would neither help him to disentangle their fellow citizens from the mortal coil in which they lay, nor would they depart one iota from the law which forbade them, even to save the life of others, to have their dead defiled by a Jew. So, in the end, the back of the lorry was once again closed up and it drove on with its dreadful load for another twenty miles to where there was a doctor of the Moslem faith. When it arrived every man inside was dead. For this the Jewish doctor got the blame.

After so much pain and sorrow and persecution it was interesting to meet at last a man whose origin had been the same as our own, a Briton. What made him come, we wondered. We had become conscious in a way in which we had never been before of what Europe had meant in terms of human suffering in the lives of many individuals, and of what those who called themselves Christian had done to others not of their faith. It had been a sobering and humbling revelation. But surely the tale would be different when it came to our own country. Maybe something of the Pharisee's prayer was also in our minds: Thank God we are not as other men are. And yet, uneasily, I remembered the hostile whispering, the cold rejection that I had been witness of on my own doorstep. Maybe we also were not blameless.

But the answer, when we got it, was a different one, and not without its own significance.

Dan was a man in his thirties working as an Information Officer in a new town, the urban service centre for a reclaimed rural area. He had been eleven years in Israel and did not regret it.

'Why did you come?' we asked, and he told us his story.

His father, an elderly, stout, professional man, working in Glasgow had long had a dream of Zionism. He was of the generation for whom the return to Israel was a consuming passion that lit their lives with purpose. But he had not passed this on to his son, who grew up as an ordinary British boy, good at games, with his circle of friends and with little knowledge of the world outside his limited group. He knew of his father's passion, but he did not share it; indeed, when he thought about it, he felt himself to be aimless with no particular purpose or direction.

The time came when he was called up to his National Service and he went out to Egypt with the Army.

WOMAN AT THE OPERA

'Did you find any discrimination because you were a Jew?' we asked.

'No,' he answered. 'On the contrary, I was very happy, and there was absolutely no distinction made between us. In fact it was in the Army that I first began to feel that life might have some purpose.'

Egypt was an eye-opener to him. For the first time he saw the world outside his own concerns and he was shocked at much of what he saw. But it was a beneficent shock. He became interested in the lot of the fellahin, and began to wish actively to concern himself with helping those less privileged.

Then, out of the blue one day, he received a letter from his father. This was in the 1950s, and it simply said what he already knew. 'I have long wanted to go to Israel and I feel now that this is possible with assisted immigration. Will you come with me?'

His father was then fifty-two, a man who had been all his life in business, not fitted physically, whatever his spirit might be, for the hard life on the land of a new country. The boy knew that his strength and youth would be needed, and, at first, this alone seemed to offer him a purpose. So he simply wrote back: 'Yes.'

The father sold up everything, left Britain which had always been their home, and with his wife and son set out for a *moshav*, a communal village, in Israel. When they arrived nothing was as they had been promised. The land was not properly parcelled out, and all that was on it was a wooden shack behind the spot on which the house was to be built. It was a time of great austerity and hardship, but they set to to build themselves a new life. And so they had. 'I found a purpose,' Dan said, 'Something to work for. I've made money since, but money has never made me.'

We knew what he meant. We had been long enough in the atmosphere of Israel by then to recognise the difference between this land where the young were still expected to be idealistic, where their country needed them, and Britain which had ceased to give her young people the sense that they were of actual value in the building of their own community.

But there was one person in this story whose hopes and fears, and indeed whose wishes, were never mentioned.

'What did your mother feel about it all?' I asked him.

He gave me a curious look. 'Well, she came,' he said. 'But it's been harder on her. Yes, it's been hard on her.'

An original pattern of the populating of Israel had been that of the individual immigrant, pulled by a vision or struggling to escape, striving to set up a new kind of communal living which would enable him to take possession of the land. Then the matrix altered, indeed was curiously reversed, and while the individual did still arrive much of the fresh immigration consisted of groups already tightly knit on whom the impact of this new country was more likely to have an effect of disintegration. The urge that brought them was more instinctive and primeval than that of their predecessors. They were threatened by no immediate terror, nor was their driving force a mystic grail. They were unlettered and inarticulate, had they been able to express fully their reasons for coming they might perhaps have used a simple, common, universal word: home.

These were people who in their outward appearance differed very little from their thousands of fellow countrymen in the distant lands from whence they came. At least in Israel they did not appear to differ, it may be that seen in India or in Iraq we could have told at once that they did not come from the common stock. Outside Jerusalem, on the ancient, rocky, terraced hills, that do in truth give the appearance of being older than time, we saw two villages composed of people from these countries.

Driving up the bare curving road in the brilliant winter sunshine that would have passed for summer in a more northerly clime, we drew level with a girl walking. Our driver knew her and we stopped. This was Ruth, daughter of a well-to-do and widely known Jerusalem family, who was the social worker for a group of villages, of which the Kurdish village was one. She had returned two weeks before from a tour of America which had taken her over much of that country, but there was no sign that this had in any way changed her attitude to her job. We gave her a lift up to the village, and she, in return, took us into a home to visit one of her women.

These people came from Iraqi Kurdistan, and it so happened that we had ourselves been in that country and so had some idea of their original background. Physically it did not differ so very much from the conditions in which they now found themselves, and in this way they were more fortunate than some of their neighbours. Kurdistan is also a land of rocky hills, and an eye accustomed to the alternate claustrophobic closeness and great sweeping distant views of mountain country would suffer no shock when it was transplanted here. Though the village was not old, a year or two, and

48

agriculturally was only just beginning to support itself, the women looked at ease and at home in their neat, small, concrete houses well equipped with all mod. cons. They wore the full wide peasant skirt and white headscarf that seemed a compromise dress between the still unwesternised region from which they had come and the uniform cotton dress which would be their children's wear, and they spoke to Ruth without shyness or subservience.

But there were stresses and strains of course, stresses which perhaps in every village of this kind fell particularly on the women. One of these, I felt, must be language. Facility in Hebrew was a basic necessity for every Israeli citizen, not only because a common language was one of the major binding forces in the creation of a nation out of such varying elements, but also because this ancient tongue had for all Israelis a sacred significance. For the men Hebrew was an accepted necessity of life, acquired as much by daily contact in the district cooperative store, the tractor depot and the grading shed with men with whom they shared no other common tongue as in conscious learning: for the children there was no real problem, all schooling was in Hebrew and they soon forgot that they had spoken anything else. But the women were not in a like situation. Their work did not take them outside their homes and the incentive to learn was consequently lessened. Chat with the neighbours could continue unchecked in their own language. Until the day when they discovered that they did indeed have a need to learn Hebrew, the day when they found that their children no longer understood them in their mother tongue. Astonishing as it sounds this was a fact. The greatest pressure on the women to learn what was to them basically an alien language was that they could not otherwise communicate with their own children.

When we had first arrived in Israel and been greeted by Gershon and his wife, another Ruth, we had discovered that Ruth was an American. A short while later we were invited to a picnic to meet the family, Hanan, Danny and the little girl Yael. I had been delighted to think that now, at last, we should be able to communicate with some Israeli children, for up till then all the youngsters we had met had been cut off from us by the barrier of language. So I looked forward with eagerness to the fun of discussing what we had seen and done with the two boys. But it was not to be. Though Hanan spoke some English, learned in school, their only language was, in fact, Hebrew. Gershon's wife spoke Hebrew to her children and in some ways this was one of the biggest surprises of Israel. An earlier Ruth had said: 'Whither thou goest I will go . . . and thy people shall be my people,' and here again were those words most lovingly interpreted.

But to return to the Kurdish village. Social-worker Ruth told us how every now and then in her work with Jewish groups from under-developed countries she would come up against superstitions and practices which belonged to their country of origin though not to their Jewish faith. Much of Israel seemed like an unscrambling of eggs—to rescramble them in a different way! One of these super-stitions concerned the giving of blood, always among primitive peoples a matter of deep fear and concern, for they feel the blood to hold the life force, and the taking of it not only diminishes a man but may give his enemies power over him.

It so happened that in this particular village there was one family greatly afflicted by an hereditary disease, where the children, of whom there were many, frequently stood in need of blood trans-fusions. Israel within itself is not a rich country and, as with her land, it was only what was put in that could eventually be taken out. The villages must contribute to the blood transfusion service if they wished to benefit from it. This Ruth tried to explain one day to her women from Kurdistan; and here she met a resistance which was not one of logic or reason but welled up out of a deeper instinct. They would accept a blood transfusion, yes; as they accepted the modernity of their little houses, the excellent schooling for their children, the change of occupation, often, for their menfolk. But they would not give blood, even though they saw the connection between the giving and the saving of life.

The old and the new lived side by side, and sometimes the cogs meshed neatly together, so that they created a fresh whole, but sometimes the teeth failed to connect and there was a grinding, and occasionally a breaking. Of necessity change came fast because it was imposed from the outside and not of the people's own making, and naturally it was the children who adjusted themselves most quickly to the new life. Learning, opportunity, equality stretched before the young Israeli as it had not done before the young Jewish Kurd, or Moroccan, or Indian, and the patriarchial pattern of societies whose wisdom was gained predominantly from experience rather than from books began to break down. In a new country it was no longer necessarily the father who would be approached for advice in a difficulty or a crisis, rather it might be the son who understood better and more quickly the complexities of a literate society. This alteration in the ancient ways could have far-reaching effects on the social structures that many ethnic groups have brought with them to their new country, and it is not yet by any means certain what the shape of the future will be.

Even the presence of Ruth was a threat to the old social order, for the village, struggling now with an environment about which

AGRICULTURAL
COLLEGE TEACHER

it had no ancient traditional formulae, was dependent on its outside assistants, the social worker, the agricultural officer, the visiting nurse, and others, rather than on its own internal knowledge and skills. One could only admire the way in which both parties in this difficult transition attempted to achieve solutions which did no violation to human dignity.

Not far from the village of the Kurds was another with the curious and familiar name of Gestetner. Here again East and West, the old and the new, met in a fascinating combination. The village, a very new one, set starkly on top of a rolling, rocky hillside, had been established with the financial help of the wealthy, world-famous family of Gestetner and was inhabited by Jews from Cochin in the Indian state of Kerala. Their native tongue was Malayalim, they spoke it still, and in the chill breeze off the bare Jerusalem hills their fine black faces looked slightly pinched and drawn. For them the change from their lush tropical homeland was much more severe than it had been for the Kurds, and I wondered how the women, exposed as never before in their little boxes of houses which lacked any kind of softening greenery, would be able to adjust themselves to this new life. For the women, like

51

Dan's mother, do not make the choice; they go where their men take them and it is on their shoulders, unsustained maybe by idealism or a vision, that much of the harshness of the new world falls. Israel, for all the brave propaganda of feminine equality, has not yet changed the patterns of a man's world.

But here again it was the children who offered hope for the future. I went into the village nursery school, where tiny, doll-like little girls and boys conducted a kind of miniature world in among furniture cut down to size and lisped the Hebrew words that their mothers could not understand.

This village was settled. However gropingly and uncertainly at first, the taproot had gone down into the Israeli soil. But there had been a group of Indian Jews from further north, Bombay, who had not been so fortunate. They, too, when the news of the establishment of the State of Israel penetrated to their community had decided to make the great uprooting and take themselves, their sons and their sons' sons, with all their possessions on the great pilgrimage of faith to the Promised Land. But for them the promise, on a secular level, had not been fulfilled. One can imagine them, coming probably from the back streets of a busy Indian city where they had been traders and craftsmen, men long established, respected some of them for their wisdom and learning, a small group, tight-knit, feeling themselves to be somewhat superior because they were different. They sold up their homes, realised their money on the possessions that were too large to accompany them, and set out full of hope for the land of the promise.

What did they expect it to be like? One cannot tell, but I imagine that they had never considered that the climate might strike chill, the land barren and cheerless; they had not known that their traditional skills as craftsmen, shopkeepers, councillors, traders, would avail them little in a country where every new immigrant went at once on to the land, to till it and cultivate it and make it blossom. No doubt they were warned, but the effort of imagination required to relate those warnings to reality was beyond them. Maybe, also, that where once they had known themselves to be different and taken pride in it, they were disconcerted to find themselves now the same and without any special honour or distinction. Who knows: all one can tell is that for them the promise was not fulfilled and so they packed up once again, gathering together the sons and the sons' sons, the wives and daughters and possessions, and they set sail back to Bombay. But, alas, once roots are cut they are not so easily set down again. Back in Bombay they found that life had closed up after them and left little trace. Even, it may be, that having glimpsed another way of life something, after all, had made them dissatisfied with what up to now had been their own. Whatever it was they could no longer settle back, and began to talk again of going to Israel. They had had outside assistance with their passage, and their sponsors were by now beginning to get somewhat tired of their uncertainty. Like the traditional wandering Jew this little group shuttling back and forth across the Indian Ocean seemed in danger of being permanently lost, perpetually in motion. However, once more they gathered themselves together and they sailed for Haifa. This time they stayed. I imagine that by now they felt like the homelesss who are glad to grasp any possibility of home. We smiled. But looking at their brothers from Cochin, struggling to root themselves in an alien soil and an alien way of life, however much at home their spirits were, I could understand the anguish of those poor souls from Bombay. It was not in their hesitancies and distresses that the extraordinary lay; it was in the transformation of the thousands of others from many different lands that we saw the miracle.

BOY ON BICYCLE

CHAPTER IV

The Second Generation

GIRL FROM TRIPOLI

WHEN Dr Cohen arrived in Israel, not so many years ago, he felt himself to be among Gentiles. He, as a Jew, had been conditioned to being submissive, modest and inconspicuous, but now he found himself among fellow Jews who were aggressive, self-confident, pushing—like Gentiles.

He was speaking of the Sabras, those who had been born in Israel, the citizens for whom there had never been any other background, who knew nothing of what it felt like to live as a minority in a country which to a greater or lesser degree had repudiated them. Sabra: the name given to the homegrown Israeli is also the name for a common local fruit, the prickly pear.

'Do you know what they call the children who are born here?' we would be asked by middle-aged Israelis. 'Sabras. The prickly pear. Tough and prickly outside, but sweet inside.'

'Once you get there,' they would add with a little laugh.

Sometimes the laugh denoted pride in the achievement of a generation who felt themselves the equals of the world in their rights

54

and in their citizenship, but sometimes it showed an awareness of uneasiness at a phenomenon which had not been foreseen. For those who were born in Israel the world did not look the same as it had done for those who had fought and suffered from outside to establish her. No more in Israel than elsewhere does time stand still, and, as so often everywhere, many of the older generation were perplexed and fearful when they looked at the young.

'I'll tell you when a child is a sabra,' said Dr Cohen. 'I see a small boy in the street and I say to him, "What is your name?" If he says, "Mind your own business," then he is a sabra.' And he shook his head, because on the one hand he was glad to see a generation that felt no need to bow its head before the uncertain patronage of others, while on the other he deplored the respect that was gone.

It is no simpler in Israel than it is in any other country for the young to live at close quarters with a famous father or a heroic, immediate past. We can tolerate an epic history if it is sufficiently safely embalmed to leave us free to accept it, or a great-grandparent of formidable stature whose example we are under no obligation to follow, but to rub shoulders every day with those who have endured or risen to the extremes of human behaviour is a great strain on most of us. So Nahum's son dismissed his parents' past with a cheerful: 'That was Zionism. It's better now,' and went off to play football with his contemporaries unaware of the turmoil that his tacit repudiation of all that he had suffered engendered in his father's heart; and the carpentry instructor's daughter was not interested in her father's memories. One Friday evening at a family meal I was discussing clothes with my neighbour at table when she said to me:

'You know it's very awkward in the summer with short-sleeved dresses. They show the concentration camp marks tattooed on our wrists and the children just simply don't understand. But I can't wear long sleeves all the time and an operation to have the tattoo removed costs money.' She shrugged. Later she said: 'You know our children say to us, "Well, why didn't you fight? There were six million of you after all." It's simply impossible to explain to them what it was like to be in Europe during the war.'

Practically the first Israeli with whom we had any prolonged contact spoke to us with great bitterness about the young who had not suffered. He talked blindly, as if it were their fault, somehow they should have sought persecution, proved themselves to be worthy of the great heritage. And three weeks later the cry came back to him from the daughter of one of his contemporaries: 'Everything has been achieved. You fought in the Second World War, in the Hagana, for the liberation of Israel. What now is left for us to do?' For the sons and daughters of pioneers, who long for the rights and risks of citizenship, are rebels without a cause. For them the old patterns are outworn and outdated, and no longer physically even a possibility, but acceptance has not yet emerged for the fresh directions which pioneering must inevitably take if the new generation is to have the right, as it should, to create its own myths and to perfect its own kingdoms.

Nevertheless, whatever the ferments that may be stirring among the young in Israel, it still remains true that this is a society where the young are expected to have ideals, and where no one is gently cynical if they attempt to do good rather than, as in our own community, to make good. Israel needs its youth still in the old ways, for active defence and for physical nation-building, and it may be that she can profit from the failures of more aged nations in finding fresh challenges for her young people which will renew in each generation the spirit of the nation.

For the challenges are there. No country which is making the enormous experiment in human relations that Israel is making lacks for urgent, exciting enterprises. The integration of a population of such diversity of background and disparity of educational standards is in itself a mammoth task, and one on which the whole future of the country

SLEEPING SOLDIER

depends. But whether this challenge can hold for the young Israeli the same drama and urgency as the wrestling of fertility from the land or the hewing-out of a kingdom from hostility had for their predecessors remains to be seen. It is not the young who lack the enterprise to look for fresh horizons, it is the adult population who distrust their ability in ways other than the old and tried ones.

For every Israeli youngster, however, the Army is still a part of everyday life in that it claims his or her service for a considerable period of time at the age of eighteen. On the whole the claim is welcomed, and the Army is a potent factor not only in giving the country its strength against foes outside its borders, which is of course the primary concern, but also in building a unified nation out of the many heterogeneous elements. For two and a half years the young men, and for two years the girls, from every kind of background, literate, illiterate and semi-literate, live and work together at tasks which are by no means exclusively military. The Army is Israel's massive adult education programme, teaching Hebrew to all those for whom it is still a foreign tongue, and reading and writing to the semi-literate and the illiterate. Sometimes even to the literate too. We heard of young men from the Yemen who could indeed read and write, but they did both upside down, because in the villages where they had been taught there were few books, and when the group sat round the rabbi to learn, some, of necessity, had to look upside down at the book which lay on the ground in the centre of the group. The Army also inculcated country skills into young people for whom the cycle of seedtime and harvest may have been a mystery; and ultimately it welded into one unity the black, white, tan, fair, dark or red human beings who knew themselves now to have shared one common experience, to have worked together for one immensely worthwhile cause. If Israel's enemies abandoned their hostility overnight and she had no more need to defend her borders, one is tempted to feel that she would still have to invent adequate cause to retain her Army, for where else would she find an instrument so well suited to the task of the basic social development of the nation.

For a country so tiny, and at one point Israel is only fourteen miles wide, an Army which consisted in part of all able-bodied citizens between the ages of eighteen and twenty-one was remarkably little in evidence. At least doing military things. The border,

HITCH HIKER

57

which is everywhere and seems to be constantly within a stone's throw, lay peaceful and deserted in the autumn sunshine. But at every crossroads on the highways of the country hordes of young soldiers of both sexes stood hopefully attempting to thumb lifts. Sometimes it seemed that the entire call-up was out on the roads trying to get back home. I wondered if they ever did. We rarely saw a car stop or pay any heed to those patient wavers, and indeed the numbers involved tended to act as a deterrent. But they never gave up and were as much part of the Israeli landscape as rows of cypresses or groves of oranges. It seemed to indicate that Israeli long-distance buses were not very frequent or reliable and that a soldier's pay was very small. It also indicated that the Army's public image was a civilian rather than a military one. This was a citizen army, deeply involved in the life of the nation. It was not something frightening or strange, it was the boy or the girl next door, to be treated with no special deference or distaste. The Army was the nation, and the nation was also the Army for in an emergency it would take only a very short time for every single man and woman to report back to their units, ready and under arms.

There were two units which carried a special prestige value. One was predictable, the paratroops, though what was not forseeable was to be told that backward boys from a special school did very well in this unit; the other was uniquely Israeli. This was the Nahal, the elite group whose function was to start up pioneer agricultural settlements on or near the border, or to help in older kibbutzim in areas of hardship like the great desert of the Negev. After a year in normal Army training a group of young people, both men and women, who had come to know each other well and to work well together as a unit (it was possible that they might even have originally come into the Army together from a youth movement) might elect to go, as an entity, to start a new Nahal on some barren hillside where no cultivation had taken place before. Many of this group would be young people whose background was in any case rural but not all; some would be from towns, going off with a light in their eyes and a gun over their shoulders to till the soil in the old pattern that had been pioneered by their parents before them. Undoubtedly there was still a strong pull for many of the young people in the cultivation of the sacred soil, and not just simply in its cultivation but in the knowledge which was implicit in the role that the Army played in this. Every extra yard of Israel which

THE NEW NAHAL

was made fertile and eventually settled was one more acre embattled against the possible encroachment of an enemy.

But the old mould is, in fact, already cracked. We were invited to see the setting up of a new Nahal on a hilltop overlooking the border. It was to be called Mei Ami, I think in recognition of Miami which had provided some financial support. The unit had moved in only the day before and there was to be a ceremony of dedication, addressed by the Prime Minister, before they were left to their arduous task. A new road had been cut over the hills, up to the cluster of buildings which were to house the unit and form the base for the settlement. It was a rough, uneven road, but broad and well graded. Up it all kinds of vehicles, from our own private car and the cars of various well-wishing officials to the jeeps and lorries bringing representatives of other Army units to wish their comrades well, streamed in a long line. The blue and white flags flew from temporary posts at regular intervals, the buildings looked new and raw, the formica tables in the dining-room were unmarked; drawn up in two lines on the flat space that had been bulldozed out were the young troops who were to live and work here. They looked cheerful and pleased with themselves and not particularly smart. We were, perhaps unreasonably, disappointed. This was the toughest of the Army units, Israel's pride, following in the great tradition, but the years had already subtly undermined that tradition. The new road which led to the border, the new buildings which

59

crowned the hilltop, had been built by ordinary commercial contractors before the Nahal unit ever arrived. In a sense it was they who were the pioneers, using their machines where once every stone had had to be moved by hand. And the atmosphere of fête and festivity, with proud parents inspecting their offspring's bedrooms, was far removed from the stealthy, silent advance under cover of darkness which had set up the first settle-

ISRAELI GIRL

ments to make the border safe. The day will come, indeed is already forseeable, when there will not be so much land left unclaimed, and then where are the frontiers which will demand their sacrifices from the young?

Army service was an honour; rejection by the Army was also rejection by the nation, a disgrace. This could be seen in the case of the young delinquent who, if he had been in prison, would not be accepted by the Army until he had been good for a year. In some ways this seemed a great pity, for the young man who had been in prison was likely to be just the kind of young man for whom the Army could have provided a challenging remedial experience. There were few sabras among the juvenile prison population, and very few boys from orthodox, strict families. It was the young immigrant, whose whole traditional family structure had been imperilled by the impact of this new country who found himself most often in trouble, a contributory reason for which may have been the difficulty of getting worthwhile work between the ages of fourteen and eighteen because employers knew that they could only look forward to a gap of two and a half years when the call-up came through. So the mixed-up, ill-educated young immigrant, for whom the stability and influence of the Army could have been a boon, and who would have benefitted immeasurably from its programmes of social education, was sometimes the very person whom the Army would not accept. Fortunately, because juvenile delinquency rates are still low in Israel this did not happen so very frequently.

A more poignant problem was brought home to us by an Arab.

Israel has her Arab citizens too, especially in the northern area of Galilee. They live on and cultivate the lands which have been theirs, and their father's before them, for many generations. They present to the Israeli a challenge and an irritation, a reminder always of the great unsolved dilemma with which he lives. We met one day an intelligent and charming young Arab. After much talk, over cups of tea, the conversation came round to his friends. Were they also Arab, or did he have Israeli friends too? Oh yes, he had many Israeli friends. They had gone to school together, grown up together. He sighed: 'I am lonely now,' and his fine thin face grew pensive as he gazed out over the land.

'Why lonely?' we said.

'They have all gone to the Army. It is their period of service.' He smiled at us gently for being so simple as not to realise that.

This was a delicate subject and we were unsure how to proceed, but we were interested. My husband looked at the very sympathetic Israeli official who was with us and then ventured: 'Would it not be possible for you to go too?'

The boy looked at us: 'Oh yes, I could volunteer. But it would not be the same. I would not be able to do what they are doing, we would not be together.'

'If they wanted me,' his eyes said, though his lips remained silent, 'If they wanted me they would have called for me. Then I would have known that I was needed, and, better still, that I was fully accepted. But they did not do that. Now if I volunteered I would know that they were embarrassed to know what to do with me. I would go on guard duties, at places where the guard was not very important; I would serve in barracks where I could be always under observation. Not for me the call of the frontier, or the freedom of the skies. My friends are gone. Why should I be lonely in the Army when I can be equally lonely in my home?'

That there is a quandary facing Israel here is plain to see, whether they have resolved it rightly is not so obvious. For the question that nags at her Arab citizens is not just, 'Will I ever be trusted?'

which could in time and with goodwill be overcome, but 'Will I ever be wanted?' the answer to which is not so clear. Israel is a land of many peoples. The diversity, and the unity, astonish and inspire the visitor. But they all have one thing in common also: they are all Jewish. This is, or was until very recently, the overriding criterion for Israeli citizenship. The paradox is that a people who are apparently so extraordinarily various are nevertheless extremely exclusive. 'Mama certaine, papa peutêtre,' said one of our guides with sardonic emphasis when explaining to us that to be a Jew the mother must be a Jew. He then went on to describe some of the difficulties that immigrant groups had with the Rabbinical Court, which is an arbiter in such matters, when it was discovered that back in their history, perhaps in the Yemen or North Africa or in Bombay, the patriarch had taken to himself a local, non-Jewish wife. Now, for his descendants, this might well prove to have been a vital, perhaps even a fatal decision. For it could be ruled that they were not Jews, and in that case were they Israelis? There are the outlines here, as yet tentative and undefined, of what could become in time a major social problem.

The other problem raised by the young Arab was not exclusively Israeli but universal, and perhaps more properly the concern of older nations. Voluntary and compulsory are emotive words in Europe, especially in Britain, where the first is good and the second bad. But for the Arab boy, and I believe for many young people everywhere this is a false antithesis. He longed for the compelling voice which gave him no choice but said: 'Come. You are needed.' He knew in his heart that when this happened he would have a place in a community which valued him for what he could bring it. For youth, hesitant perhaps, uncertain, looking for direction to the group of which it is a part, wants to establish its own identity by answering the call of the community: 'It is here that you are of value. Come and help.'

But life is a shifting, moving, creating experience, abhorring any form of static. There was in Israel a community which said just this to its young people, in the strongest possible terms, and yet we did not feel that it had wholly found the secret either. The secret of allegiance may be, but an allegiance which was inward-looking and to some extent stultifying, rather than outreaching and growing. This was the kibbutz, the communal settlement.

The history of the kibbutz in Israel is much more complex at close quarters than the outsider imagines, and the political affiliations of various kibbutzim are an elaborate jigsaw puzzle which I, for one, never succeeded in putting together. But the original philosophical ideas behind the kibbutz movement were not difficult to grasp. The land, the holy soil, was a symbol of all that other peoples have ever felt was contained in the word 'Homeland', but it was also much more. The union of the people and the land, after so many centuries of dispossession, contained also the elements of a spiritual mystery which was to bring to birth a third force, not a nation only, as others were nations, but a unique regeneration of a way of life.

In the beginning there was not much else but the land, some of it unpromising stony soil, and so these early fathers of the gathering-in would have had in any case to turn themselves from professional men and traders, urban dwellers in ghettos, into rural farmers tilling the soil. But they did not do this in a spirit of bare necessity, they did it with a positive exaltation. To go with this union of the people and the soil there must also be a new way of living, freed from the trammels, the hypocrisies and the deceits of the old life which they had left behind. A way of life which released to the maximum the common spirit which each man felt to flow so strongly within him, which liberated all his energies for the tasks in hand, and which gave every soul an equal stake in the life of the infant settlements and in their defence in time of trouble. All material goods were held by the kibbutz and distributed to its members as their need required. This was true also of all money. Services were common to all, food cooked and eaten together, children cared for and taught in their own special home so that the women, equally with the men, were able to give the full eight hours daily of work on the land. Life was hard, simple, austere, but the compensations were also very great. Within the kibbutz a spirit grew up of interdependence and of a depth of reality which made the urgent individual preoccupations of the outside world appear vain and trivial. What mattered was the community, and submerging their separate identities in the group they found strength and satisfaction.

This was pioneering, treading a path both physical and sociological which had not been trodden in quite this way before. The standard of education and culture in the kibbutzim was very high; it was an elite who elected to follow their ideals in this fashion, a second choosing of a chosen people. The ground that they broke, whether it was the actual soil of Palestine or in the realm of social custom, was fresh ground. The buildings they erected, whether the houses in which they lived or the ramifications of group living, went up where there had not been such structures before. The crops that they harvested, whether the growth was vegetable or spiritual, grew where no such crops had ever grown. The kibbutzim looked outward and saw that what they were doing was good and could set a pattern for a new nation.

But in time there grew a second generation for whom the kibbutz was not an exciting pioneer experiment, but home — safe, established, cosy, and on the whole not something they much wanted to share with other people. The kibbutz could hold its own youngsters and it could still attract young people from overseas from whom it now had romantic connotations, but its diminishing manpower could no longer be reinforced from within Israel's own borders. Gradually a cleavage was coming to exist between those youngsters who had known no other background than a kibbutz, and those who knew the kibbutzim as part of the myth of Israel but had no desire to look closer than that. And in the young kibbutzniks, splendid-looking physically, fair, tall, upstanding, there were apparent less pleasing qualities of arrogance and indifference towards those outside their orbit. 'We used to call them the Tnuva Boys in our unit,' said a young Army Officer. Tnuva was the co-operative marketing organisation responsible for selling the kibbutz produce. The kibbutz boys in this particular unit used to receive huge parcels of food at intervals containing the best, and it was very good, that the kibbutz produced. This in itself would not have produced the nickname, what did that was their unwillingness to share any of this fare with those who came from outside their own immediate circle.

It is never easy to be a stranger in a land which is not one's own, and perhaps less easy at this moment in history than it has ever been. The strong stirrings of nationalism in the world make for sensitivities and guilt complexes which bedevil ordinary friendships and distort simple communication. The situation is a curious one, for the more interdependence is thrust upon us by our own technical expertise the less we seem able to accept that we have any humanity in common. The one place in Israel where we felt this twentieth-century tendency to prevail was among the kibbutz children. Of necessity our meetings with them were few and superficial, but the barriers between us, the unseeing look which deprived us of shared human experience, spoke of a society which was satisfied to be insulated from those outside.

The behaviour of the young Israeli overseas makes a curious counterpoint to this. Studying in Europe or America it would be natural to him, at least so his parents think, to gravitate towards the Jewish communities which still live in these countries; to find his friends among them; to make his home with them. But this does not happen. It seems to have become more normal for young Israelis to eschew the Jewish element and make their friendships within their universities with other young people of similiar age and tastes to themselves without reference to religious background. When asked: 'But why did you not spend your time with those of our own people?' they will reply: 'Them! But they are not like us. We are Israelis.' Perhaps along with the pride of country there is an un-conscious — or conscious — repudiation of those who had a choice, who could also have been Israelis but chose not to be.

In the days of the great persecution in Europe the Youth Aliya was set up, in 1933-34, in an attempt at least to save the children. This was an organisation which arranged the emigration of children alone, without parents or friends. It was a kind of Jewish children's crusade, not to rescue the Holy Land but to people it and to save the young life of the future nation. Many of these children went into kibbutzim, which needed the manpower and which were ideal institutions for a child who had no family or roots of his own. All kibbutz children lived together in any case away from their parents, and it was the kibbutz itself which became their family as well as their home: every parent was their parent, as every man within the kibbutz was their brother.

Still, though in a much reduced form, the Youth Aliya continues, but now more often it is the parents who send out little Benjamin or Moshe, as Noah sent the dove and the raven out of the ark, to discover if the land is really there and to test it out.

We went up one day to a village above Haifa, Ramat Hadassah, a children's village which received all the unaccompanied children under sixteen who arrived on the shores of Israel. Once there had been four such villages, now there was only this one, and here they spent about two months accustoming themselves to a new country and a new life, and being shaped by that country into the kind of citizens that it required. Here they learned that 'To work means to help,' a lesson that, surprisingly enough, was needed particularily by those from the eastern European countries, notably Poland, for whom even to work was apparently a hard lesson. We had always imagined that the children from communist regimes would at least know what work meant. They lived in small units with houseparents and all the work of the house, the kitchen, the laundry, the garden was done by the children themselves. Here they were closely watched and assessed so that they could eventually be fitted in to the most suitable background, and here they learned the ethos of the community to which they had come. It was not always a simple task. There were problem children, and children with problems. From Poland, Turkey, North Africa, South America or India they came, sometimes suddenly and unexpectedly, sometimes, as from South America, with notice of their arrival and plans carefully made. Some were small, and much could be done with a smile and affection; some were big, and had already the sense of pride and responsibility which would turn them into acceptable citizens. It was the in-betweens who were not so easy. For them freedom might go to their heads, while at the same time they feared the demands of being on their own. Or the freedom, which was the freedom to work, might not be what they had imagined, and that the work was mainly of an agricultural nature could be an alien idea to a teenager from the backstreets of some urban slum.

Standing on the verandah of the cottage which belonged to the twelve-year-old boys we were greeted by a mischievous, dark-eyed little rogue. 'Shalom,' he said, which means peace, and he turned his flappy Israeli linen hat round on his head and squashed it into a very recognisable shape, then striking an attitude with one hand tucked into the bosom of his shirt he cried 'Napoleon' and grinned at us. Conversation stopped there for lack of any more common words, or we would have liked to have found out why he chose to greet us with an imitation of the little Emperor, whose hills are littered about this part of the world in much the same way that Queen Elizabeth's beds are scattered over England. We asked where he had come from. 'Spain,' they said. 'The family hope to follow him in time, but he has been sent on first to find out what the country is like and what opportunities there are, and to report back.'

We looked again at that cheerful twelve-year-old face.

'It must have been a wrench for his mother,' said my husband. 'How could she ever bear to let him go, alone, such an enormous distance. What must she have felt as she watched the ship pull away from the dock?'

We smiled at 'Napoleon' who gave us a wink. Whatever the new life held for him he looked ready for it.

Moshe's parents, along with the rest of the village, had been cave dwellers in North Africa. That is, they had inhabited from time immemorial rock dwellings, gouged out by nature or by generations of human hands, from rocky cliffs and hillsides. When first they arrived in Israel they had not known how to live in those nice new houses. No doubt they felt unprotected and precarious in the extreme, exposed on all sides to wind and weather and the approach of possible enemies. It is said that when the social worker came to the village the morning after the people had been settled in she was surprised, and even somewhat alarmed, to find it quite deserted. The

neat houses lay empty, their sparkling newness unsullied. Then, gradually, at her approach, people did begin to emerge, coming out from under the houses where they had dug themselves temporary shelters which at least resembled the homes they had always known. But that was some time ago, for Moshe was about nine or ten, and he had been born in Israel.

That was the trouble, so his parents said. The old disciplines which had buttressed a patriarchal society were broken now, Moshe who went to school, spoke only Hebrew and was learning skills his father had never known,

MOSHE'S FATHER

and now, to the shame of his parents he had stolen a sum of money from the school and the police had been called in. Nahum told us that this was very rare. Small, close-knit communities like this could generally solve their own problems without recourse to outside aid.

It was father who recounted the tale, slowly and with much help from Nahum in gentle probing questions. He was a fine-looking old man with a lined weather-beaten face and he spoke of his son with cheerful common sense. But the mother could not face the situation with quite such equanimity. She sat in a corner weeping and ringing her hands, comforted at intervals by a neighbour. Moshe we never saw. He was said to be at school, but when we called at the school and were received by the headmaster Moshe's name could not be found on the books. Somehow he seemed to have slipped out of the social pattern and no one quite knew where he was. Maybe it was easier to step into a new world of your own volition and adapt yourself to it like our small Napoleon than it was to be the first of your family born into it like Moshe. For him the old mould was irretrievably broken, but he had had no part in the breaking of it and merely found himself bewildered by the two facets of his inheritance.

That same day, driving along the main road, we saw at the end of a long line of hitching suppliants, mostly soldiers, a small boy. We stopped and picked him up. This was Shalom, whose origin was Yemeni, and who lived in a Yemeni village very close to the border indeed. He came from a religious background and wore the small circular cap on the back of his head which was mandatory for all orthodox Jews. Two thin corkscrew curls hung down on either side of his alert olive face in front of his ears. He was going home from school. Because he came from a religious sect he went to a religious school, and this necessitated a journey of some miles. He had missed the bus home at two o'clock, and the next one did not pass the crossroads for an hour or two later.

'What would you have done if we had not given you a lift?' I asked.

'Waited,' he replied, without any sign of annoyance or surprise that so many hours should be added on to his school day.

'When do you leave in the morning?'

He named some very early hour, which enabled him to catch the bus even if it did leave him with plenty of time to spare at the other end. But he did not worry. He was near enough a Yemeni background to value immensely the opportunities that were now open to him and to have no feeling that time was in any way a commodity that had to be conserved, or used, or dreaded. It was simply there, like that air one breathed and as little regarded.

We let him out at the end of the road that led up to his village. The country was flat, broken by small stony hills. The border, which lay close in front of us, looked very peaceful and there was no sign at all of any military activity. On the other side a white Arab village crowned a rise and glittered in the late sunshine. The slender minaret of the mosque rose up into the blue air. A man on a bicycle came by who had been attending a court case concerned with some boys stealing oranges. It was difficult to believe that enmity existed in such a pleasant land.

'Abba,' said Hanan to Gershon, 'Can we visit the wool factory?'

As always when we heard the Hebrew word for father we started. It seemed to us so familiar, and yet we could not get over the feeling that it was somehow faintly unseemly to use it so lightly in this everyday fashion.

We were going on a picnic on Saturday, the Sabbath, with Gershon's family, but first we were to visit the new port of Ashdod

ARAB VILLAGE OVER THE BORDER

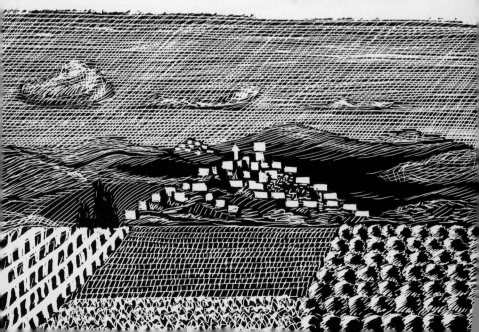

FOOTBALL AT ASHDOD

which was growing up out of the sand dunes of Tel Aviv. It was
rising in defiance of all natural features. There were none. The coast
was straight and without indent or shelter, cliff or cutting. The bare
sand ran back from the sea in banks. Underfoot it shifted and sank
with no apparent stability at all. Yet directly out of this sand great
rectangular blocks of flats dominated the horizon between sea and
sky, and in front of them on a level sand pitch the Ashdod football
teams, in their yellow and black jerseys, played soccer with the
same skill and abandon as anywhere else in the world. Down on the

foreshore the chug-chug of a little train indicated where the new breakwater was being laboriously built up to offer shelter to the ships that were to come; and along the strip of land, or of sand, which lay between the water and the road several great gleaming factories, with huge metal chimneys and bright orange girders, grew proudly out of the hot, bare shingle.

Hanan, like other boys of twelve elsewhere in the world, was fascinated by the machinery and the power that these factories represented. Once before, on a picnic to this same spot, he had had the luck to be taken in to the wool factory, and now he was determined to go again.

Gershon was not so sure. It was the Sabbath and the factories were closed. Ashdod, too, was still only half built and we were, after all, foreigners. It might be that we would not be welcome if we were discovered peering, however innocently, at the latest methods of wool-processing in Israel. For the first time I saw him slightly discomfitted on our account, afraid that we might be put in a position of embarrassment. But Hanan had no such qualms. He revealed then that on the previous visit he had taken a photograph of the watchman's small son, and a print of this photo he had now armed himself with as a bribe to gain access, an earnest of our genuineness.

Gershon's pride in and desire to please his son won the day and we drove, somewhat hesitantly, along the levelled beach road to the factory gate. There was no sign of anyone, but under Hanan's guidance we climbed out and made for the door. Suddenly two boys materialised out of the air. Hanan's friend, about the same age as himself, and an older brother. It appeared that they were watching the factory for father who had gone to the synagogue. Hanan produced his photograph and it was agreed that we should be allowed in for a conducted tour. The door was opened into the office quarters and we passed through.

At that moment there was a hitch. The younger boy seemed suddenly to take in that we were foreigners, and to feel that after all he owed some obligation to the absent father. Seeing the hesitation and sensing what it was about we hastily consulted together as to what proof of identity we could bring forward to allay his fears. My husband had nothing of any real value, but I had my passport with me. This we produced and the boys, after scrutinising it earnestly, agreed that we could pass.

We were then taken into the factory proper. Huge steel doors

71

were rolled back and there, in an enormous shed, the whole process of preparing Australian wool for a commercial market was laid out before us. The smaller boy proceeded to take us on the most efficient and knowledgeable conducted tour. He knew, and could explain, the function of each machine. He berated us for dawdling, gathered us up like some small sheepdog when we seemed inclined to stray, or to disregard the proper order in which the machines were ranged. He turned on lights here, and even, to prove a point, a machine or two there. He looked like a small ragamuffin, but his confidence was supreme and his pride in his factory complete. We could not have had a more persuasive or interesting guide had the public relations officer himself been on duty. But where else in the world, we asked ourselves, would it be possible to find a factory left in charge of a twelve-year-old and at the same time find that twelve-year old fully conversant with the entire process of the machinery which he was guarding? To find a small boy whose background was of primitive Morocco, talking to strangers about up-to date twentieth-century mechanics with complete poise and confidence? Some of the paradoxes of Israel were clearly displayed here.

The older boy, who had not accompanied us round the factory, came to join the party as we emerged again into the sunshine. He spoke English, which his small brother did not, and we engaged him in conversation. It emerged that he spoke also six other languages. He was a clerk with Leylands, studying at night for university.

'Where did you come from?' we asked.

'Morocco.'

'When?'

'Myself? Seven years ago. But him,' he indicated the younger brother, 'two and a half years ago.'

'Why was that? Did you come alone?'

'Yes. Do not ask me why. It was personal. My mother died and I had to come.'

'Were the things bad for the Jews in Morocco?'

'No. No. It was not bad. It was personal.'

'What would you like to do?'

He shrugged: 'Psychology — something of the sort.'

'And your brother?' we asked. 'What would he like to do?'

'Oh him! He is obstinate. No one can make him do anything. Not even wash.'

72

It may have been so. It did not surprise me. That small boy knew where he was going and would not be easily deflected.

The girl from Venezuela was very pretty. She had red hair and a skin with the bloom of a rather dark peach. She was a student at a famous agricultural college, and when we met her she was laying the table for college lunch with a group of cheerful, attractive girls in jeans and shirts. The girl from Venezuela was called over to talk to us because she spoke our tongue, and we were surprised when, having started the conversation in rather stilted this-is-for-foreigners language, she replied in perfect idiomatic English.

'Where do you come from?' we asked again.

'Well, really Trinidad,' she replied.

'Trinidad!' we exclaimed, and in that exclamation there must have rung clearly overtones of a special relationship. 'Trinidad. But that's not Venezuela!'

To our consternation her eyes filled with tears which began slowly to trickle down her warm, peach-bloom cheeks.

'No one here knows where Trinidad is, or has ever heard of it,' she said, and the wavering smile she gave us indicated that at that moment we might almost have belonged to her own family. 'I have to say that I come from Venezuela to make it easier.'

'How long have you been here?'

'Seven months. I came in May.'

'Alone?'

'Yes, alone. My parents wanted me to come, so I came. I've an aunt and uncle in Israel. My parents may come later. It depends.'

'Do you like it here?'

Her great brown eyes still swam with tears, but her smile had grown stronger. 'Fifty-fifty,' she said, and one sensed the loneliness and homesickness for a far-off West Indian island which struggled with a feeling of adventure and achievement.

'Do you speak Hebrew?'

She shook her head. 'I am learning,' she said. 'It is difficult.'

'What will happen when you have finished your course here? Will you go into a kibbutz, or work in a village?'

'Oh no,' she said. 'I want to be an air hostess.'

When we had left her the agricultural officer who was our guide said to us: 'Perhaps if she had not shown traces of her negro blood her parents would have sent her to America. But maybe in the circumstances they felt she would be safer here.'

73

Many of the strands that compose immigrant young Israel seemed to be intertwined in this one girl: the mixture of blood that offered no security anywhere else in the world; the struggle to reorientate an entire life and to base the new one on a strange language; the friendship and acceptance of the group, many as mixed as she, into which she had come and the surging homesickness for the friends left behind; the basic training in agricultural skills on which the land had been founded and made fertile and the intended rejection of this way of life for the glamour of an air hostess; the urge of parents, at whatever sacrifice, to make possible for their children freedom and independence in a land of their own.

SABRA: PRICKLY PEAR

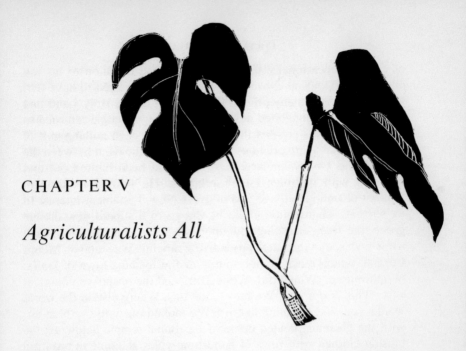

CHAPTER V

Agriculturalists All

OUR visit to Israel was made at the urging of a friend in the Ministry of Agriculture. It was natural therefore that everything connected with the land as a living, productive, fertile unit should have bulked large in our programme. However, this emphasis on the soil is, in fact, an important part of the Israeli mystique, and we should probably have been immersed in it anyway, though not perhaps in such depth and with such knowledgeable instructors. Each day saw us going out with a different guide to experience some facet of the task of making the desert blossom and the stony places bloom.

At first this was somewhat of an intellectual strain, for our own agricultural knowledge could conveniently be lodged on a sixpenny piece and we had no wish to appear to depreciate our hosts' generosity with their time and their wisdom by foolish and futile questionings on our part. Our interest in all they showed us was very real, and I soon learned how to give it an acceptable form by gently probing one day's expert in the area of knowledge which would be revealed to us the following morning. In this way it was possible to arrive forearmed with some reasonably sensible queries which saved us from both rudeness and embarrassment.

Very early on the stage was set for us, and we were given some inkling of how this land was regarded by our first guide. He had been French, but had left France some thirty years before; a man of caustic, occasionally bitter, tongue whose devotion to his job and to Israel was all-consuming. He would have liked to have felt, as would indeed many others, that the soil of the Holy Land had been a blank, uninhabited desert before its own people returned to it. Or, if that was not possible, that there had been nothing in it of any merit, that every previous sign of human endeavour between the time of the Dispersion and the 1940s had been blotted out and replaced with worthier Israeli projects. He hurried us through villages of undoubted age and of great New Testament interest to us so that our attention could be drawn to a superb new orange grove, the trees marching row upon row, piped for irrigation, each trunk encased in the latest protective wrapping. We stood on Mount Carmel, which looks grandly out over the teeming town of Haifa: he murmured, 'Wonderful. Wonderful,' and the unspoken comment was, 'This is our city. We have done this. Where else in the world would you find anything like it?' We looked out into the blue air, with the gleaming golden dome of the Bahai temple below us; the hillside clothed with rows of handsome villas standing in beautiful gardens; the port beneath us, the shining silver drums of the oil installations; the blue sea and the long curving line of the coast which ran away to the ancient port of Acre on the opposite horn of the bay. It was a magnificent sight. But we knew, for we were British, and our fathers and brothers too had fought in this land, that a major portion of what we saw had been here before ever the State of Israel came into being, owed much to the British or was actually built by them.

'It's a wonderful sight,' we agreed politely, but we were alienated by the lack of generosity; the more so because there was no need for it. Israel had indeed so much to be proud of and the miracle of growth and production, of afforestation and reclamation, was apparent even to our untutored eyes.

'It was covered with rock and they planted trees,' our guide said, gazing across a wide plain protected on all sides by rounded stony hills, and this time the pride and the passion in his voice aroused in us only sympathetic emotions—though some short while later we found it difficult to resist pointing out that a hundred-year-old olive tree in a grove through which we were passing could not possibly be disguised as a post-Independence phenomenon!

Later the conversation turned on the British hankering after the romantic.

'You have never liked us, the Jews,' said Mr C. with some bitterness, 'because we wore collars and ties. You prefer the Arabs with their flowing robes. The picturesque, the feudal, that's the British. Pah!'

He drove even faster, disdaining for once to point out a new village of square white houses shining starkly on the hillside. For this moment we were generically British and could not be expected to appreciate anything modern and up-to-date. Abashed we sat silent, examining rather guiltily our own consciences and coming to the conclusion that he had just made a gross overstatement.

At that moment we rounded a corner and came on a flock of goats cropping the rough grass at the roadside. In charge of them a small shepherd boy with a staff in his hand wandered slowly along. In his white head-scarf and his long grey robe, with oval olive face and great dark eyes, he represented time immemorial.

'O stop!' cried my husband. 'Please can we stop. I'd like a photograph.'

Then we looked at each other appalled. This was it. We had shown ourselves true to our heritage. No new villages or orange groves had engaged our camera, but at the first sight of a wandering child with some goats we were ready to disrupt the whole timetable — and he had to be an Arab!

'Goats!' said Mr C. more bitterly than ever. 'They should be wiped out. They destroy the land.'

We were to spend the night in our first kibbutz, Ayelet Hashahar, north of Tiberias. We came down on to the Sea of Galilee just as the sun was setting, bathing the Syrian hills on the opposite shore with a wonderful pinky-orange light and reflecting the flamingo sky in the quiet waters of the lake. It was just the Sabbath, Friday evening at sunset, and Tiberias, which is a holy city, appeared deserted. All transport had stopped, and only we, Gentiles driven by an agnostic, broke the law. Away to the north lay the line of the great new pipe which was to take the waters of the Jordan to help raise the desert of the Negev from the dead.

'They fish at night here,' said Mr C. surveying the sunset with satisfaction because it was showing what Israel could do. 'There are very bad storms on this lake. It's dangerous. Sometimes the Syrians shoot at them too,' he added as an afterthought.

We remembered, almost with a sense of shock, how some fishermen who had fished all night and caught nothing had been told to go out again and cast their nets, and had brought in a miraculous draught. And of the sudden storm that blew up while the Lord slept. They still blew these storms, and the fishermen still went out at night; time snapped back and forward with an astonished recognition of reality. But we did not say this to Mr C. who was always somewhat affronted when we displayed any knowledge of his country's past history. Instead we said: 'It must be an uneasy life right on the border, never knowing what is going to happen next.'

He shrugged: 'Why? We never think about them.'

Ayelet Hashahar, when we arrived at it after dark, had been specially chosen to be our overnight stop because it was a kibbutz which catered particularly for guests. In fact it ran the best guest-house in Israel. In many ways this, which was intended to be its great advantage, was, for us, its big disadvantage. As with many outside visitors to Israel the word 'kibbutz' evoked in our minds a particular image composed partly of admiration for a dedicated social experiment, partly of the glamour of an unknown way of life, and partly of a kind of preset antipathy to communal non-private living. Before we left London I had said to my husband: 'I can stand everything except the girl's dormitory! I really feel I'm too old for that!' and this fear on my part typified the kind of stereotyped habits of thought, built more often round personal likes and dislikes than based on any real knowledge, which forms the outsider's judgement of the kibbutz. Nevertheless we also recognised certain philosophical concepts, the sharing of worldly goods, the treatment of all men as equals, the renunciation of a capitalist economy, and we approached our first kibbutz with mixed feelings which included some desire to find our prejudices justified, but also I think a real longing to discover a genuine step forward in human relations, a contribution, however small, towards solutions of the complex social problems which beset us all.

With a flourish we drove through a gate and came to a halt outside a brightly lit and very modern building. Beautifully kept gardens could be dimly seen about us, and down a path behind flowering shrubs and fruit trees several more luxurious blocks rose into the evening sky. It was all very unlike our ideas of a kibbutz! We knew, however, about the guest-house run by this old-established and very flourishing kibbutz as a kind of off-shoot from its main agricultural preoccupations. It also ran a canning factory in a nearby village. We piled out of the car and looked for someone to show us where to go and to assist with the baggage. Mr C. disappeared into the main building to make enquiries and off a bench, where he had been curled up asleep, a man rose grumbling and shuffled over towards the car. He looked at our bags without much sign of eagerness, but eventually, when Mr C. returned, was persuaded to help carry them across to one of the bedroom blocks. It was the off-season and there were very few guests.

The room we were ushered into had everything for which a guest could wish. It was simple, but contained every sort of convenience that modern living could devise: lights, heat, the self-contained bathroom with boiling water, all were perfect. It was very far removed from the girl's dormitory of my previous imaginings! So too was the meal which we presently ate in a dining-room beautifully decorated with growing plants and cunning glass screens. In the morning, when we drew up the blinds, we looked out on to a flat plate of land, highly cultivated with fruit trees, vegetables and other produce and surrounded by the round, stone-covered Galilee hills.

It was a wonderful place to stay: but it was not a kibbutz by our terms of reference.

There were several disturbing anomalies. The evening before we had gone into the kibbutz proper, which lay behind the guest-house, and we had walked around its rows of small houses in the company of a young man who lived in one of them. But there was no real contact between ourselves and the kibbutz members. The young people were rehearsing an evening entertainment in the enormous

GALILEE HILLS FROM AYELET HASHAHAR

communal dining-room. When we heard the music as we approached another preconceived idea had flashed across our minds – that we might perhaps dance with them. Some Israeli group dances are famous and a matter for national pride. We climbed the stairs quickly to see what was going on. It was a curious sensation when we walked into the huge room. The sixteen-year-old age group was gathered at one end, some performing the rest sitting around watching them. We might have been ghosts lurking unwanted on the fringes of the party. We longed to speak to them, but our guide warned us not to and looking at their faces we could see that for them, indeed, we simply did not exist. They might run a guest-house as an admirable paying proposition, but the contempt which they felt for its users struck cold across the barriers.

That there was a barrier was not simply a product of our imagination. This kibbutz was now encountering problems much more subtle and more difficult of solution than those of the early settlers. Prosperity brought its own menace; as affluence had once corrupted the monasteries, so riches threatened the philosophies of the communal settlement. Ayelet Hashahar employed paid labour in its canning factory and this was totally at variance with the original conception of communal working and sharing. But the years of hard, dedicated effort on the land had borne fruit, both literally and metaphorically; the kibbutz was increasingly productive but production had outstripped manpower. There were various courses open among them, to retain the basic fundamentals considering the actual social experiment more important than the products of its fields and work only within the limits of existing manpower; or to consider the kibbutz' output of major importance for the Israeli economy, which it was, and make up the deficiencies in manpower with paid labour. The dying attraction of the kibbutz as a lifetime's devotion for young Israelis seemed to rule out an intensive recruitment of full members. Ayelet Hashahar took the second of these alternatives, but it suffered, so it seemed, from a guilt complex for doing so which made the community retreat from open recognition of any shared ideals with those whom it had, perforce, brought into its orbit. We would infinitely rather have lived in simpler surroundings, eaten less exotic food, and shared the companionship and gaiety which undoubtedly existed within the kibbutz itself.

In the course of conversation with our companion he introduced a subject which particularly interested me. It was the difficulty of finding enough employment for the women. Freed from all private domestic chores, and without the responsibility for the upbringing of their children, they were ready and willing to work alongside their men. But the hard truth was that the work which presented itself to them was primarily the shift to public domestic chores and, for a few, communal work with the children. Some did work in the fields, and seasonally, as at harvest, all were needed, but it was manpower that the kibbutz was short of for the hard heavy work of the soil, and it seemed that no real solution had been found to the problem of the women.

Suddenly I saw that I had been too harsh in my, unspoken, condemnation of the guest-house. Here, of course, was the outlet for the women, and an admirable one. Here their special talents and their energies were also productive for the kibbutz as a whole. I said this with some warmth.

There was a silence. 'Oh no,' replied the young man. 'They do not work in the guest-house. Inside the kibbutz we are all prepared to do any job that the community needs, and there is no feeling that some kinds of work are less worthwhile than others. But that is different. The women would not like to wait upon outsiders.'

With a feeling of depression I realised we were, after all, all human, and that even here solutions had not yet been found. The fine concepts operated within the chosen group, but in the real test as to whether this group could take out into the world the truths that it had discovered there was as yet little sign of success.

We left Ayelet Hashahar the next morning to drive in a huge arc north and round again to the sea at Acre. We hurried past interesting archaeological remains and holy cities inhabited by orthodox sects, to whom our motor car on the Sabbath would have been an offence. We saw the spot where an attacking Arab force had been put to rout by a trick of enormous noise in the night; the harsh new villages gleamed in the sunlight along the contours of the pink and rocky hills; the trees grew where no trees had grown before; the myriad stones that cumbered the soil were painstakingly transformed into sturdy, stable terracing. The huge cutting which was to take the Jordan pipeline south to the desert reminded me of Tel Aviv and the notice in every bathroom asking guests to save water and remember the Negev. In spite of this I had indulged in an enormously deep hot bath and

I was never wholly free from guilt thereafter! Mr C. had mellowed. his suspicions of our innate hostility had been allayed. He cursed the five-day week — 'an invention of the devil' — and decided to let us have a look at the fort at Acre. Perhaps he had converted us, perhaps we were never the stereotypes that he had expected, whatever the answer we felt as we watched the hordes of multicoloured children, who clambered about on the enormous obsolete guns that overlooked the sea, that it was the living Israel which held most fascination for us at this moment.

Some weeks later, driving towards a border village, we passed through a small kibbutz whose cow sheds and grain stores lay on either side of the road. On impulse we asked if we could stop and visit. Our guide on this occasion, a young man of great charm and simplicity, said, 'Of course,' and stopped the car.

This was a very different contact from our first encounter with a kibbutz among the hills of Galilee.

When we had walked through the byres, gazed at the cattle which gazed solemnly back at us, smelt the strong, satisfying farmyard smells and seen something of the hard, compelling routine which is indivisible from an agricultural life anywhere, we asked if it was possible to visit one of the homes of a kibbutz member. Our guide, who was as much a stranger to this kibbutz as we were, walked with us along the neatly edged paths where two-roomed dwellings were scattered about a grassy space containing one or two communal buildings. We looked for a house which was occupied at this time of the day, late afternoon, and at last he spied one on the far side of the settlement. We stood outside and he raised his voice and asked, in Hebrew, if there was anyone at home.

A young woman, plump and fair, with reddish-gold hair arranged in one thick plait which lay over her shoulder, came out, to be joined presently by a man of the same colouring as herself. When they heard that we were strangers who were interested in the kibbutz movement they smiled at us and said: 'Come in, come in.'

We walked up the little path and entered the tiny, but immaculately kept and beautifully furnished, small house. Everything was gay and modern and reflected an individual taste, from the aquarium along one wall to the low tiled table in front of us on which the wife had placed a bowl of clementines. They pressed us to sit down and she offered us a cup of coffee which we accepted.

'Could we ask them some questions?'

Our guide translated this request into Hebrew and the young man smiled and replied: 'Certainly.' I had the impression that he had been through this process very often before and could probably have told us what it was that we would ask before we did so. But he showed so signs of boredom or annoyance, and he talked with thoughtful simplicity.

'Could we know then how long he and his wife had lived in a kibbutz, and whether they had met each other there?'

Our guide conveyed the gist of this. The husband glanced with affection at his wife, who had just come in with more fruit and some biscuits.

'We are both sabras. We met each other in the Army during our national service. We both volunteered to go to a Nahal, and when our time was up some of us, who had been together in the Nahal, decided to continue together in a kibbutz. It was then that my wife and I got married and we have been here ever since. We have three daughters. The youngest is just two months old.'

At this moment there was a small squeak from the other room and the wife came in with a very tiny baby which she handed over to her husband. I was extremely interested. The position of children in the kibbutz is one of the most controversial features, and even the kibbutzim themselves are not all agreed upon this issue. Originally the children were totally separated from their parents, except for two or three hours each day at set times, usually in the early evening when work finished. Otherwise they lived, slept, ate and worked together in a children's house, under the care and supervision of one or two trained members of the kibbutz. On the Sabbath, and on holidays, they spent the day with their parents. This freed the parents, especially the mother, for 'productive' work alongside the other members of the kibbutz, and, so it was said, made for a better relationship with the parents because the children saw them only when they were relaxed and at ease. The father, in particular, probably spent a good deal more time with his children then he might in the rush and pressure of an affluent and commercial urban society.

Some kibbutzim, however, had begun to feel that there were unforeseen facets to this educational theory. Against all logic many of the women remained dissatisfied and frustrated, and the first generation of kibbutzim children proved to have problems and frustrations of their own. It could be that the constant company of one's peers is not, in fact, the ideal upbringing for a world which requires us to form relationships between the generations as well as within one's own age group. So some kibbutzim have returned to allowing children to sleep in their parents' house one night a week, the night of the Sabbath.

Here, however, in the little house in which we sat, the traditional arrangement held good. The mother had had her baby with her, at home, for the first two months, and the very next morning as it happened, the infant was to go into the Babies Home so that the mother could return to her job in the clothing store. From that time she would see her, as she saw her other children, only for two or three hours each day. Watching her comforting the baby as it whimpered a little in her arms I could not help thinking that freedom to do the job in the clothing store, issuing new clothing, repairing the old, exchanging and listing, did not sound adequate compensation for handing over one's child for other women to feed and comfort and train.

At this moment the father said to us that it was time for him to fetch his other two daughters for their playhour with their parents. When they came, two small girls of about three and five, they were overcome with shyness at the sight of three strange adults and clung to their father and mother hardly daring to look at us.

We had explored rather tentatively the matter of money, which is entirely a communal affair. How did they decide about holidays, for example? Did the kibbutz say what price the hotel room must be? No, he said, the kibbutz, which meant the meeting of all the members, decided on an adequate sum for holidays and it was then a matter for each person to make his own arrangements in a way which fitted in with this sum. I remember that we felt the sum which they mentioned seemed pitifully small, but they cheerfully explained that there were various ways of stretching it; they could go to relatives, or even perhaps to another kibbutz for some of the time, and of course

NURSERY SCHOOL CHILD

their own kibbutz had information about places where it was not expensive to stay. If, for some special reason, they wished to go further afield, to Europe perhaps, or to spend more, then they must ask permission of the meeting and explain the circumstances. We later met a man who had received a large sum of money as German reparations. This he had handed over to the kibbutz of which he was a member, being allowed, however, to retain enough to take him on a trip to Sweden. As for clothes: they were allowed so many new things a year and this was perfectly reasonable. I looked at the young wife's attractive cotton dress and she laughed as though she had read my thoughts. Yes, at first the clothes for the women had been dull and stereotyped, but gradually as the kibbutz had got more established and more prosperous this had changed. The clothes were pleasant and up-to-date and they had a wide choice.

We came away admiring. Sturdy, stable, settled, they seemed to have built a life that they found wholly satisfying.

We were, in fact, on our way to visit a moshav shitufi, which is the other form of village co-operative settlement in Israel. The services in a moshav are centrally administered, marketing the crop, any processing that may have to be done, buying seed or provisions, storage, light, water, perhaps a tractor station; but each family unit has its own land, lives privately in its own house, earns its own money and keeps any profit, in the way that families have traditionally lived for a very long time. It seemed an ideal combination of the old and the new, of the retention of individual initiative while drawing strength from communal effort. Of course there were difficulties, in what area of human life are there not difficulties, and one of them was also a problem for all Israel, the actual shortage of land. The units in the moshav were not large, and so highly cultivated was the country owned by any moshav that expansion was simply not possible. So when families grew up and sons might want to stay in the village of their youth this was not always a practical proposition. The kibbutz could use all its children on the large communal single unit that was its land, but the moshav,

PICKING FLOWERS FOR EXPORT

which was the more natural unit for the new immigrant to turn to, found itself constricted by sheer lack of available ground. If a man died, or a family left the moshav, priority for the vacant plot would go to a member of the younger generation belonging to the village. But while family land could use and support one son, especially when the father grew older, the others would probably have to seek their way of life outside the hamlet, maybe helping to start up a new moshav in a less developed part of the country or in urban jobs, from which they nevertheless returned constantly to the enriching family background of their own village. When driving around the countryside one is struck by the intensity with which every inch of the Israeli soil seems to be cultivated. Nothing is wasted or fallow, there are no sprawling woods or rolling open hillsides inhabited only by birds and sheep. Settlement is not only a matter of economic survival it is also vital to the country's security. True, in the south there lies the great desert of the Negev, an area about a third of the whole country, as yet sand and new towns and mineral industries, and plans and dreams of fertile blossoming. But even the Negev, whose reclamation is still in the future and full of special problems, does not answer a questioning gradually gaining strength in the minds of Israeli agriculturalists: what is to happen when there is no more land to pioneer?

The other basic problem is water. Israel, unless and until she can make use of the sea for this purpose, has very little natural water. The Jordan is her only river of any size – and the Jordan water is disputed water. So each village, each kibbutz, each holding however big or small, has an allocation of water that must be strictly adhered to, and upon this water more than upon anything else of sun, or soil, or man's ingenuity, depends the whole pattern of agriculture. It is the life-blood, the vital necessity upon which everything is founded. Water becomes suddenly a precious commodity, not to be lightly used and left to drain away, but to be bathed in with a proper sense of proportion as to the relative value of one's own body and the needs of the earth. It is fitting, perhaps, that one of the significant images of the Israeli townscape should be the hot-water sun-heaters, the aluminium-painted drums with their angled mirrors, marching row on dazzling row along the flat white roofs.

Our tea party in the kibbutz had delayed us somewhat and so we arrived at Kfar Hess, the moshav, after dark. Kfar is the Hebrew for village, and this was a large village whose centre and symbol

86

was the grain silo which soared up into the sky topped by the menorah, the seven-branched candlestick.

We bumped over the muddy track, for it had rained recently and the village roads were not made up, to the house of Zvi who was our contact. He was the man responsible to the Ministry of Agriculture for those foreign students who were sent to gain some insight into how this kind of village community worked by actually living in it. At this very moment it was a group of young Mexicans who were, so to speak, in residence and we hoped to see something of them.

While waiting in his house for Zvi to appear we looked at the shelves of books which rose from floor to ceiling on one side of the living-room; and we were struck again, as we had been in the house of Nahum, the probation officer, not only by the scope and depth of literary interest but by the range of languages. Here were philosophers in German, beautifully produced Art books in English, novels in Russian, poetry, drama, history, essays, with the alive, used look that books have when they are lived with and read. One would not normally associate this kind of library with a village farmer. Indeed Israeli village farmers are unique, for many of them are men who are not village farmers at all, but have chosen to become so bringing with them the riches not only of wisdom and experience but also of learning and interests gained in quite other spheres. It is not an uneasy compromise; there is no feeling of nostalgia for a better life left behind. Zvi emphasised several times that he was 'only a farmer', and it was obvious he said this because it was in his farm that his heart lay. Driving us round the orange groves he pointed to a man working among them: 'That's the Prime Minister's public relations officer,' he said. They are good farmers, this is at once apparent even to the most uninitiated, and they have remained at the same time men and women who are in touch with the arts and the politics and the philosophies of their own country and of other lands. The blend is smooth and complete, the flavour satisfying, and it is this very thing which enables them to make one contribution to the developing countries which is pre-eminent. Young men from Africa and Asia who are growing up in territories where there is a destructive paradox, that the land which is vital to them is yet despised as an occupation by those who consider themselves educated, see here plainly demonstrated that it is possible to be an educated small farmer, to work with your own hands on your own fields, or even on fields which are not strictly your own in the sense of being your individual property, and yet possess intellectual and cultural interests which would not be out of place in a sophisticated urban society. It is a salutary lesson.

Zvi, when he came, was a small dark man with a sharp thin face. He had had a life of many uprootings, beginning in the Crimea, going from there to Turkey, where he had been a petty official, then to Palestine and the dangerous unsettled life of the Army. Now, in Kfar Hess, he had found at last a place to put down roots and his son, physically one of the most beautiful small boys that we had ever seen, was born in freedom and had never known the kind of total insecurity which had been his parents' lot when they were young. Some time later Zvi was to take us into his back yard, where the hundreds of battery chickens that seem inseparable from any Israeli settlement squawked and chattered in their tiny cages, and show us the garden shed in which he kept his tools. It was the normal small wooden shed which fulfils such a function equally in Britain.

'It was in here,' he said, 'that we lived when we came to reclaim this land. We are prosperous now.' He looked round at his modern, well-designed house with the lemon trees growing by the front porch, the long rows of hen houses, the orange groves in the distance, and then back to the simple wooden shed. 'We lived here, in this shed, while we created this with our own hands. We do not forget.'

But will his son also remember?

We arrived on a day of fiesta, the Anniversary of the Mexican Revolution. The Mexican students were this evening entertaining all those who had been kind to them to a 'pantomima' in the training college nearby. Would we come too? Certainly, we were only too delighted to have the chance. Well, the lorry left at seven, there would just be time for us to meet our hosts for the next three days and to change if we wished to.

Up to this moment we had not been certain where we were to stay. Now, as we collected our two small suitcases, Zvi said: 'I have the tractor outside. I will take you down to the Edelsteins.'

MULE CART

88

We had not bargained for a tractor, which is a precarious kind of vehicle on which to travel if two of you are passengers with baggage. Perhaps it was good that it was dark and many of the more perilous aspects of the ride were hidden from us. The other form of transport in Kfar Hess seemed to be a small wooden mule cart and no doubt this could have been equally uncomfortable. There was an extra saddle seat at the back of the tractor and on to this I installed myself, with some difficulty because my skirts were not shaped to climb over enormous farm machinery wheels. My husband sat perched on the mud-shield which stuck out at the side. Thanking our stars that we had for once managed to travel really light, we each clung to an overnight bag.

In the headlights the mud gleamed oozily thick in front of us, and every now and then with a flat, slapping squelch great pats of it would fly up around us. But there was no time to worry about the possibility that one of these might get misdirected. Every physical effort, every tensing of nerves was required to keep the body upright on the bouncing, shaking, mercilessly hard, iron seat. It was not far to the Edelstein's house but the body that clambered stiffly down when we arrived there seemed to have had its skeleton entirely rearranged in that five-minutes ride.

Mama Edelstein had opened the door and an oblong of bright light streamed out. She stood smiling, a small, square, grey-haired woman, welcoming and homely. Once inside the clean, neat house we discovered, however, one snag. Neither she nor her elderly husband spoke any English. They were of Polish origin, and their languages were Polish and Hebrew, with a little German. Our German varied from good, my husband's, to invented, my own, but we all had one thing at least in common — a desire to communicate and a willingness to make efforts, however ludicrous, to do so. The Edelsteins, who were simple unsophisticated people, were accustomed to entertaining foreign visitors to the moshav and found it an interesting experience. They had a son, Avram, who was gradually taking over the land from his father, and for whom, and the fiancée he hoped soon to marry, an extra room was being built on to the little house. Avram spoke fluent English, and he would come in once a day, Mama Edelstein explained, to answer any questions we might have and help with any problems that cropped up. She beamed in a motherly way on us and retired into her kitchen/sitting-room leaving us to prepare for the 'pantomima'.

ARAB VILLAGE FROM KFAR HESS

Promptly at seven o'clock a ten-ton lorry drew up outside our temporary home and Zvi came in to ask if we were ready. In the lorry were fifteen or so Mexican students, clad in their best suits, young dark faces split by very white teeth as they smiled at us. In the cab Mrs Zvi sat beside the driver and I was told to climb in with her. Ten-ton lorries are not the most comfortable form of transport, but after the tractor ride it felt very civilised.

Kfar Hess lies very near the Jordan border. From the top road of the village, which lay along a spine of land, the line of demarcation can be clearly seen, except where orange groves run parallel on both sides of the frontier. Then one wonders whether in the secret green glades Jew and Arab ever come face to face and, hidden from the public pressure of their fellows, greet each other as farmers of a common crop. But, whatever happens in the orange groves, Kfar Hess suffers sporadically from raids which can have deadly consequences; and no doubt the Arab village on the other ridge could say the same. Zvi told us how, returned after dark from working in outlying fields or visiting a nearby settlement, he would hesitate between taking the nearest way, a track which passed close to the border, or the long detour by the main road—and take the detour. Mrs Zvi said how anxious she became when darkness fell and she knew that her husband was coming home with this choice of route. She feared, each time, that his desire to get home quickly might outweigh his caution, and she could not rest until she heard his footstep on the porch. There had been two boys ambushed one night who had not come home, and even in the village itself, though lying just on the edge of it, a farmhouse had been blown up by a bomb killing the young couple who owned it. Prosperous and peaceful it might all appear but death still stalked in the hours of dark.

It did not seem so at this moment. The Mexicans were singing, songs of their own country interspersed with some they had learned in Israel, and in the cab the driver was asking hungrily for news of England; and expressing openly his delight in speaking English.

This was both a pleasure and a surprise. We had been liked without reference to our nationality, we had been disliked in spite of our nationality, we had been disliked because of our nationality, but this was the first time we had met someone predisposed to like us because we were British and for no other reason, someone whose nostalgia for all things English made him long to speak that language with a native whose mother tongue it was. Yet he was not English himself. He was a Palestinian, born in the Middle East, who had served in the British Army and risen to the rank of sergeant in the Royal Engineers. This period of his life held for him a glow and warmth that nothing which came after had surpassed. His wife had been in the A.T.S., and though she bore with his passion I do not think she shared it.

He insisted that we take tea with him next day, cajoled and bullied till it was impossible to resist. He would come for us in the lorry, which he owned and used as a means of livelihood: he must

91

not miss this chance of speaking English to us, of telling us of all the things which lay so close to his heart, and which I daresay he was finding it increasingly difficult to tell to his fellow countrymen. To love the British is not a fashionable activity at this moment in time.

So we went. It might have been pathetic, but he was a man of robust physique and forthright views, as befitted a former sergeant, and he relished our presence too much for there to be any room for patronage or pity. We saw his Army belt, decorated with a wonderful display of badges, each of which he could accurately describe; he showed us photographs, brown and faded, but still evocative of the world he loved; where others had described, with tact or flourish, how they had fought against us and outwitted us, he told with love how he had stood beside us in some of our times of crisis. It was an experience which had become strange to us — and we enjoyed it.

But it was not all time past. He had made friends in those happy days with an Englishman, then a private, I think, or some non-commissioned rank, and every Christmas since they had exchanged news and cards. The Englishman went into politics and began to make a name for himself, his friend in Israel watched with pride and admiration. There came a day, years later, when he received a note telling him that his friend was coming to Israel with a political mission and hoped to see him. Could he come to Tel Aviv for a meeting at the Dan Hotel? Filled with pleasure that this man, now so important, still remembered the old ties, he took particular trouble to prepare himself for the meeting. The Dan Hotel was Tel Aviv's finest-polished, sophisticated and extremely expensive. For this occasion he must put aside the Israeli informality which was his usual style, the hotel and the known habits of the English demanded something more of him. So he bought himself a new tie, and in his best suit, the jacket pressed and buttoned, he at last looked round the exotic lounge where the fountains tinkled and the tropical trees swayed in the air conditioning. Suddenly he heard his name, shouted in a familiar voice remembered plainly after all these years. He turned, and there coming towards him as though time had stood still, in open-necked shirt, the sleeves rolled up, jacketless and hat-less, was the English Member of Parliament whom he had come to see! They scrutinised each other for a moment, and then the Dan Hotel reverberated to their laughter.

It was good to know that his confidence had not been betrayed,

92

that the comradeship he remembered had indeed withstood the test of time.

Lightning had begun to flash on the horizon behind the orange groves. There was a storm coming up and much more rain. The lorry stopped among the handsome buildings of the training college and the Mexicans jumped out of the back. We all crowded downstairs and into the small concert hall. There were already a number of other people there, friends and well-wishers from Tel Aviv, more Mexican students from other moshavim, and some important men from the Ministry concerned to show the students that their recreations had also official blessing.

MEXICAN STUDENT

To our disappointment the 'pantomima' did not turn out, as we had hoped, to be songs and dances done by the students themselves and showing us something of the culture of their own country. Instead the items were performed by an Israeli guitar group and an extremely skilled and entertaining mime. Only at the end, just before we all retired to the dining-room to gorge ourselves with food and drink and photographs, did one of the students, an unsophisticated farm boy uneasy in his best suit, stand up and make a speech in honour of 'The Day of the Revolution'. It was long, and only his fellow countrymen understood it, but we clapped and cheered and felt for him when he forgot his lines. Then the Mexican Ambassador, who was the guest of honour, went up on to the platform and embraced the students one by one, slapping them on the back as he did so.

Next morning, in blue jeans and white sweat shirts, with conical blue Israeli hats perched on their dark heads and sleepy-eyed from overnight excitement, they looked very young and simple as we met

93

them going about their jobs in the moshav. They were genuinely farmers from rural Mexico, not urban students learning agriculture, and language was a difficulty for them as they spoke only their own. One of them, Salvador, produced a small English dictionary in an attempt to make some conversation possible, and when we took it to find a word for him we saw written on the fly leaf: 'Salvador from Ruth.' Then we remembered how the social worker, met in the Iraqi village above Jerusalem, had told us of her journey home by sea from America and how, on board the ship, there had been a party of young Mexicans bound for Israel. She had taken them under her wing and tried to help them, and to one who had particularly attached himself to her she had given a small English dictionary. Then she had described how the young man had become jealously possessive, embarrassing her by his attempts to prevent her having anything to do with other men. Her name was Ruth, surely this must be the young Mexican and the dictionary. We described her and our meeting with her and his face broke into a handsome, flashing smile. That was his Ruth who had given him the dictionary.

I had reason later in the day to be grateful to the Mexicans. Zvi came down on his tractor to offer us a ride round his fields to see the day's work under way. Prepared this time for a rough ride, I nevertheless burdened myself with some drawing materials in case there should be the chance to make pictures. We started off at the co-operative shop, where the women were doing their housekeeping and discussing the news of the day; we saw the grading shed where the fruit that was coming in from the fields was sorted into sizes and packed for the market, the grain store, the hardware shop where spare parts for machinery could be had, tools bought and everything from a packet of nails to the latest in irrigation appliances be obtained: we visited the village community centre, which could be turned into a modern cinema and saw the lecture rooms where the Mexicans had their theoretical instruction, and the quiet garden outside with the memorial to moshavniks who had died in border raids, photographs of fine-looking young men and women for whom the moment had come when this was territory to be defended rather than land to be cultivated. We drove past the nursery school, where tiny infants played and learnt under the sympathetic eyes of two young teachers, then we turned away from the residential portion of the moshav towards the fields which lay around it.

We bumped and slithered down sticky mud-paths between groves of trees beginning to hang with golden fruit, and long fields filled with tomatoes and other crops. It had rained the night before very heavily and the air was fresh and clear, but beneath the tractor wheels the earth stuck gluely. Above the roar of the engine I could hear little of what Zvi was shouting to my husband, and most of my time and attention was concentrated simply on retaining my seat on the tiny iron saddle on which I was perched. We twisted and turned, in and out of groves, around sharp corners where the tractor groaned and shuddered. All sense of direction was long since lost and all intelligent appreciation had finally disappeared. At that moment I eased the hand which had been clutching my sketch-books in my lap, and knew instantly as I reapplied its pressure that something was missing. One of the books, the one that held every drawing made in Israel up to that moment, was gone.

I looked back in the hope that I might only this moment have dropped it. A vain hope. I could not tell where it had gone, nor how far back on the churned and puddled track it lay. It was a small book and could so easily have already been pressed into the soaking soil. I thought of stopping Zvi, and recognised even as I thought of it, how a busy man would regard being made to turn in his tracks and search—for how long—for something which a woman should never have had with her if she had had any sense, far less dropped. I thought I knew the total impossibility of explaining to either Zvi or my husband the extreme importance of that book to me, because I had not known myself quite how important it was until I knew it had gone. This was something irreplaceable, a bit of myself that there was no way of ever retrieving. So I said nothing, and the day, which had been fresh and cheerful and full of interest, became a blank.

A half hour later we ground up the road towards the junction beside the Edelsteins' house. At the corner stood a Mexican student his hand raised to stop us. I knew before we got to him that a miracle had happened, he had found my book. Zvi and my husband, having no idea that it had ever been lost, were astonished at the shout of joy I gave when we drew to a stop and he held it out to me.

The last day of our stay was a Friday and as the day drew on preparations were being made for the Sabbath which runs from sun-down on Friday to sundown on Saturday. The Friday evening meal, with special food and a meeting round the table of the family, is an important one. Mama Edelstein, with whom we had grown to

PAPA EDELSTEIN

have an understanding which was no less real for being based on rather uncertain German, was making a particular kind of fish dish, gefilte fish, that was popular on the Sabbath. After it we ate cheese, and a cucumber and tomato salad – a staple in Israeli diet because they grew these things in such abundance – and clementines and coffee. At no meal did we ever eat milk products and meat at the same time, for this was forbidden by the Law, and the Law still held good in modern Israel. For the rest of the evening we sat round the small table and stretched our little stock of conversation, while

Papa Edelstein read his paper, breathing heavily and occasionally falling quietly asleep. We went to bed early, and had a night much disturbed by jackals, whose weird, unearthly call rose up unnervingly out of the darkness under our windows. In the morning, when we came for breakfast, Papa Edelstein told us, almost casually, that there had been an item on a late news bulletin which said that President Kennedy had been wounded in an assassination attempt at Dallas, Texas. Presently there would be another announcement and we would hear more. For a second the world seemed to shake. It was not possible. There must be some mistake. Then the news came on the air and we gazed impatiently at Papa Edelstein's impassive face while the incomprehensible Hebrew went on and on.

'He is dead.' He told us in German 'Assassinated.'

Mama Edelstein clucked sympathetically, and the news droned on. For the first time we felt very far from home and in a strange country. In that one moment the world changed and we could not see what the future might be.

Yet it was a carefree, happy day. The Sabbath seemed to give some kind of respite, as if it would delay both the reactions and the consequences that might stem from this day's news. We picnicked with Gershon and his family on shining sand beside a kind blue sea, far removed from any of the channels which might have brought us further news. It was only when we returned that evening to Tel Aviv and, walking to a cafe in one of the main squares, saw a newsboy selling a special issue of the Jerusalem Post, the first time in its history that this famous paper had appeared on the Sabbath, that we knew that this was not a bad dream but a terrible reality. The waitress in the cafe leant over our shoulders to read the news and shared with us her sorrow and revulsion; on the flat roof of the American embassy a solitary marine stood beside the flag at half mast.

Yet not everybody grieved. The next morning in the paper shop of the Dan Hotel, that same lush hotel which had seen the meeting of our Army friend and his M.P., where we had gone to get an English paper, we found ourselves at close quarters with a group of middle-aged American matrons. In deference to their tragedy we drew back to let them have attention first, and I listened to their buzz of conversation. It was a shock.

'Put Jacqueline in widow's weeds,' said one, 'It's a push-over for the Democrats.'

'The thing that really worries me,' replied her friend, 'is what's gonna happen now to my stocks.'

.   .   .   .

We had seen something, however fleeting, of the kibbutz movement; we had spent a little while in a moshav, but in both cases they had been old-established, flourishing settlements that we had visited. Now we were to go south, following the creeping boundaries of reclamation as they gradually pushed green fertility towards the great desert of the Negev. The first stop was Kiryat Gat, a new town in the centre of a development area called Lachish, where Dan, who had come with his father from Britain, was the information officer.

Lachish was a semi-arid area which in 1948 had had only five kibbutzim on it, as much for defence as for development, for Lachish bordered on the Gaza strip where constant infiltration took place. Then in the middle 1950s there began an explosion of new immigrants, from Hungary, Rumania, Yemen, Iraq, Tripoli, Morocco, who had urgently to be settled somewhere, somehow, and Lachish was next in the plan for development. In the eighteen months from October 1955, twenty-one villages, twenty-one moshavim, came into being.

Their composition was mixed. Twenty per cent of the new population were veteran Israelis, young Army Nahal groups or the second generation from older moshavim; forty per cent were new immigrants, not those who had come directly from their own countries to this place, but immigrants who had been already for some years in reception camps, and whose morale for this reason was low; the other forty per cent came straight from ship-to-settlement; plunged without a moment for thought or nostalgia into the day-to-day problems of their new country.

Of course this was not a simple operation; one can surmise, in fact, that it was an undertaking of enormous complexity, for here at one and the same time new and barren land was being cultivated, with all the difficulties that that implies, and a whole new, strange population was being settled, strange not only to their own country, its climate, its agriculture, its food, its ways, but also in many cases to each other. Patience and expertise in dealing with people was required as well as constancy and skill in the management of the soil.

The area was planned with a central town, which was to be a service town for the surrounding villages. This was to be a rural based economy, with the town subservient to the country. In the early days of Israel new villages of this kind had been mixed in their population. It did not occur to anyone to do anything else, there was no room here for outside national interests and no one had ever thought that Jewish immigrants would be other than idealists, prepared to accept certain hardships for the sake of a social concept. Any other identity that they might bring with them would be completely submerged on first contact with the Israeli soil. But when large numbers of immigrants from Asian and North African countries began to arrive it quickly became apparent that this was not going to happen. In the daily life of a multi-lingual village difficulties mounted, and the more this happened the more the immigrants blamed the Israeli government and set their faces against learning Hebrew. Particularly for the women was language a problem. So much was new and strange; for her the daily chores inside her own home had become suddenly unfamiliar and frightening. Water coming out of a tap may appear to be a simpler way of conducting domestic affairs, but if all your life you have gone with your friends to the well it is a lonely, impersonal, somewhat alarming substitute for this daily meeting and gossip. The children were learning strange customs, even a strange tongue which was gradually but inexorably separating them little by little from their parents; there were many moments when a wave of homesickness for the country she had left swept over the mother and she longed to put the clock back and return to the old ways. If, as well as all the frustration and effort which was her daily lot, she could not even pour out her heart to her neighbour in her own tongue then the dice was too heavily weighted against her. The neighbour who needed to be a friend might well instead become an enemy, and tensions which started with personal frictions could grow into wholesale dissatisfaction with authority which in turn completed the vicious circle by a refusal to co-operate in learning the new way of life.

So a different plan had been adopted. The villages now were ethnic groups, each homogeneous, gaining support and courage for the great adventure by the retention of a common background, a shared tongue to resort to in times of stress, and some known customs which tempered the strange with the familiar. But the villages were built round a District headquarters and here were all the services which they needed for survival. The shop was here, the tractor station, the co-operative marketing facilities, the District officials' offices, the school, the dispensary, and here the language spoken was Hebrew, which was the only common denominator connecting all those from different villages who met to transact their daily business at the centre. For the women small groups were organised to teach them in their homes, which was for them the natural environment, and these groups were taught by school teachers in their free time, or by married Israeli women who volunteered for this pioneering work of adult education. In the school children from a dozen different origins might sit side by side, learning the same things, being taught in the same way, and gradually coming to accept that they were all citizens of the same country.

Kiryat Gat had carried this conception one stage further. The rural District headquarters had now become a town, equipped with light industries. But essentially it was intended to remain subservient to the countryside enabling a flourishing agricultural economy to retain local control over every aspect of its own production from the field to the market or the tin. In the early days of the Lachish development the new settlers had arrived to find the land already apportioned out and a team of instructors, many volunteers from other areas, to meet them. The plans were there on paper, but virtually nothing had been done on the ground. On each holding a hut stood, equipped with the basic necessities of life: bed, food, some money. Some of the settlers put their belongings on top of the beds and slept under them. 'Where is the well?' they said, and were not compensated by water taps. It was important at the very beginning that there should be hard work to do and the land could not necessarily offer this all the time. Between seed time and harvest there was a long slow-growing period. So each man worked as a hired labour on the construction of his own house. This gave him both a purpose in life and some earned cash to keep his family on. But it was also essential that he should not grow accustomed just to living on a government subsidy; the instructors were 'social' instructors with a basic knowledge of economics, rather than agronomists, for this was a country geared to people who did not know its language. When the time came the new immigrant was sometimes reluctant to change his status and assume the responsibilities — and the hazards — of an owner-occupier. This new form of agriculture was a much more complicated affair than he had been used to.

At the start this was a real problem and all kinds of ways of combating it were tried. One of them showed a profound knowledge of human nature! The agricultural instructor, who acted as a kind of foreman, found his role somewhat changed. It was announced publicly that, owing to the reluctance for historical reasons of the new settlers to settle, the government had decided to control the land and run collective farms. The instructors then denounced this as exploitation. The immigrants were being cheated of the ownership of land which they had been promised. There was a demonstration and a considerable amount of indignation was engendered against the government which then ensured that when it 'gave in' and changed the arrangements the men were more than willing to take on their farms!

So, gradually and not without growing pains, both the land and the people developed together. There were many difficulties, for this was a mammoth venture of faith. These people came often from poor and depressed groups in their original countries and it was not easy to get them to accept the responsibility of local government or for co-operative endeavours connected with marketing, the tractor pool, the distribution of water on which the difference between success and failure hung. They became attached to their instructors and relied on them for more than just teaching. They were Orientals, accustomed to expect little from the world in which they lived, to subsist on a very low standard and to have large families. The Europeans had as little agricultural knowledge when they arrived, but they had a driving energy, a desire to create. Not so the Oriental for whom the sun, with its ability to make life both very simple and very slow had been a major factor.

At first the fact that he asked very little was a distinct advantage. There was no crisis period during the early months while he struggled to adjust himself and the land slowly and secretly worked its own miracle of creation. The crisis was of a different sort and came later when he was established, safe, but content with standards of production which did not satisfy the Israeli spirit. 'How can we make them expect more?' said Dan. It was a curious query.

And what of the town? It was still an amorphous place without character, built round a large central square. The buildings were flat and uninteresting, as though someone had deliberately tried to deprive the town of any glamour or attraction. It paid lip service to its function as a support to the countryside, but there were signs of uneasy stirrings in its consciousness and a half-shamefaced knowledge that it too could function in its own right. It was growing rapidly. Originally it had been planned to be a town of twelve-thousand inhabitants but already it had far passed that mark and was on the way to having a population of nearer eighty-thousand. Large subsidies were given to attract industry, and it was not in the nature of industry to remain constantly subservient to the country. Kiryat Gat was growing and beginning to stretch its sinews. It was still the service town for a rural district, processing the rural products, groundnuts, onions, tomatoes, cucumbers; canning the fruit that grew in ever increasing abundance round its perimeter; providing a scattered population with the materials that they could not grow or create themselves. But at any moment the town was going to develop a character and individuality of its own, and when that happened the balance, until now weighted in favour of the country, was going to begin subtly to be altered.

So far the values and priorities of Israel had ensured that the pull would be a rural one: unlike Britain there was a psychological conviction that on the land life was 'real'; for the young the acceptable uniform was that of faded jeans and small cotton hat which denoted an intimate connection with the soil. For us 'real' life is somehow felt to lie in cities, and the acceptable uniform, whatever shape it takes, is one of sophistication. Both these attitudes introduce judgements which are of inferiority and superiority. The test which was approaching Lachish was whether it was possible to build here an equality between town and country, each contributing to the whole society those things which it was best suited to create and yet retaining a mutual respect. It is to be hoped that this state can be achieved. Israel is entering a phase of urban development, and it may be that the Negev will alter the pattern of social occupation by providing ultimately not so much more land for cultivation as large-scale industrial expansion. Israel has much to teach the rest of the world in her attitude of mind towards the land, if she could add to this successful exploration of the relationship between town and country she could well put us all in her debt.

One last word from Dan as we said goodbye to him on the steps of his office. We had been speaking of the days when Israel was Palestine and immigration often illegal. Dan had been talking of widespread use of judicious payment to the man who might be able to pull the strings which often succeeded in obtaining an entry permit when all else failed. Then he smiled and looked out over the enormous area which was Lachish:

'But any problem that can be solved by money isn't a problem,' he said. 'If we want a swimming bath for this town it would be simple enough to raise the money. What is much more difficult is to bring the parents to agree to mixed bathing in it.'

GUAVA

JERUSALEM THE GOLDEN

CHAPTER VI
Jerusalem the Golden

WE WERE shown Jerusalem by a man who loved it. He was an American Jew who had come to Israel from affluence not through persecution or suffering but because his soul yearned to live there. All his life he had longed to go up to Jerusalem, as his ancient ancestors had done, and now, at last, he was there. This lifelong devotion, much of it from afar, when only literature and history could bring him closer to the place of his desire, had given his knowledge of the city a depth and perspective which, combined with his passionate affection for it, made Jerusalem memorable to us. He was intelligent and articulate and could clothe a bullet-scarred ruin or a barren hillside with words and imagery which brought them immediately into historical focus. He did not so much tell us what he knew about Jerusalem, he talked to himself about a city that he loved – and we listened to him.

His name was David, and he was a Professor of Social Welfare.

Though he had a long history of assisting Jewish immigrants in the days when it could be illegal to do so, and had helped to buy and provision ships from the U.S.A. in connection with this work, David himself had not succeeded in coming to Israel until comparatively recently. It is much more difficult for a man to extract himself and his family from a comfortable, prosperous environment for the sake of a dream or an ideal than it is for a man to come from a background of poverty, anguish and destruction with nothing left to him but the hopes which lie before him. The doubts which have been burned out of the minds of the latter by his ultimate rejections can still flourish and whisper among the thoughts of the former. Those who flee take their friends with them and all are of one mind, but the friends of the man who comes from a nation of tolerance and prosperity may pose strong arguments for his remaining where he is. And if he is married and has a family there may be moments when he wonders if he is taking his children to the perils of an ancient world rather than the safety of a new life. The sheer physical arrangements too are not so simple for the man who comes from a settled, accepted routine. He must divest himself of his property, pull up his roots, disentangle his affairs from their myriad human as well as business relationships. No ruthless oppressor does this for him, his worldly goods have not been carefully hoarded and protected against a possible day of judgement, but have been spread out without anxiety among the community in which he lives.

All this David did, and the time came when, with his wife, he sailed for Israel and life in a kibbutz. Seeing them in the sophistication of university life in Jerusalem one could imagine that it had not been easy for them to find themselves sharing a hard, arduous, communal life of pioneer rural agriculture. Then something happened which called out a deep obligation common to both their heritages. Back in America the wife's mother needed them. So they returned. They pulled up the roots that had begun to grow in a new country and because of the strength of family ties they went back to the old. They were away a long time, several years, and during this time David began to feel that his dream would never be fulfilled.

'I doubted whether we would ever manage to return a second time,' he said.

But they did. Eventually the mother died, and again they packed their possessions and came back, this time for good, to the country that had been their goal for so long.

They had a son, Ronnie, an intelligent small boy of nine or ten.

'What would you show us in Jerusalem, Ronnie, that your father has forgotten?' we asked towards the end of our stay. The answer was totally unexpected: 'My bedroom,' he said. 'My aeroplane models!'

All my life I had sung a hymn which began 'Jerusalem the Golden with milk and honey blest'. I do not know about the milk and honey but it was sufficient of a miracle to find that Jerusalem was really a golden city. It lay among the summits of its hills, and the wonderful mellow glow of the buildings was reflected back from the rocky slopes which for so many centuries had provided the stone which made them. However strange and harsh the shapes of the new architecture it had one thing in common with the old: the warm, honey-coloured material in which both were created. The new Jerusalem owed this to the British. At a time when the city was their responsibility, and when modern, synthetic building materials were beginning to be well known, the British perceived that the abandonment of the local stone was going to throw thousands of Arab stonemasons out of work and create a sizeable unemployment problem. So they forbade the use of any building material within the city limits other than the traditional Jerusalem stone.

'Without the British we might have had none of this,' said David with a smile as we gazed out over the new city, tawny in the evening light. 'When the war came and Jerusalem was being besieged and under heavy fire it was the fact that the walls were made of such hard rock that saved many of the buildings. Less durable materials would have been utterly destroyed.' He paused, then he added: 'We have a saying from the Talmud: "God prepares the remedy before he sends the disease".'

It was, paradoxically, in Jerusalem, where we felt conscious, almost for the first time, of an atmosphere pregnant with history and permeated by a sense of continuity and endurance which scaled down contemporary troubles, that we came face to face with the reality of Jewish-Arab relations. For Jerusalem is a divided city with a broad swathe down its centre which is No Man's Land.

On the edge of this piece of desolation the barbed wire runs, choking up every alley and lane, festooning along balconies and over shuttered windows, climbing like some flowerless rose bush around pillars in the open spaces. To the stranger whose orientation is not yet complete it seems to be always there, never was a border so all-pervading; turn unexpectedly round a corner and there it is, climb a hill and the eye is immediately across the forbidden line, gaze outward from a viewpoint and half the view is Arab. It seems both silly and irrevocable, as if to cross would be the simplest thing imaginable and the most impossible action one could take. Life goes on in a perfectly ordinary fashion with no outward sign that this is not a whole city, but constantly in the mind a bewildered curiosity twists and whispers: What are they doing over there? One stares across the landscape looking for signs of life, and is astonished when one sees it to find that they too look like ordinary human beings going about their daily business.

All old Jerusalem lies in the Kingdom of Jordan. A walled city, tight and compact, dominated on the Israeli side by the ancient Tower of David, it seemed surprisingly small. From the high steeple of the Y.M.C.A. its lineaments could be easily traced, a town within a town its outline circumscribed, all features except its roofs concealed by the encircling ramparts. But between it and us there lay a valley which we could not cross. Physically we could probably have managed it with a good deal of trouble and the acquisition of pieces of paper from the embassy, but something stopped us from taking

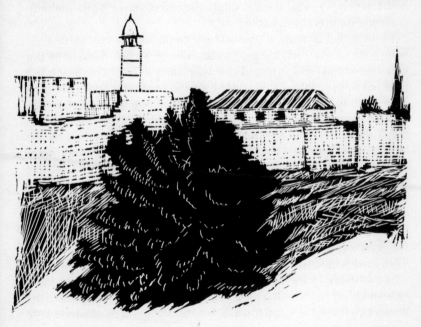

DAVID'S TOWER

this step. We were visiting Israel with Israeli friends, we could not go sight seeing across a line which might mean life or death to them.

We drove up to the most southerly point of the narrow corridor of Israel which ends in Jerusalem. There on a height is Rahel Ramat, a kibbutz which has been truncated, cut off from most of its fields by the line of demarcation. The large building which was their dining-hall still stands, its walls pitted by shell fire, gazing defiantly out of blank windows over the valley where the Egyptians came up from the south and were repulsed. The war is modern, but the over-tones are ancient, and the stubborn remnants of the kibbutz, who hang on defying any enemy to deprive them of the land that yet remains, live and work not only in the tradition of the early kib-butzniks who went about their daily toil with a rifle in one hand and a hoe in the other, but also of the remnants who remained and inherited in their own biblical history. 'They feel so bound here, so true here, that nothing except victory or death is thinkable,' Gershon had said to us about his own people, and in those stubborn, bowed backs working here on the very line itself one saw a vivid illustration of what he had meant. For us it seemed that there must surely be some way out of the dilemma; for them this was not only the Prom-ised Land, it was also the last ditch, the end of moving on—and any compromise was unthinkable.

From Rahel Ramat on one side we could see the city spread out before us at our feet, eastward the hills of Moab rose above the Dead Sea, pink and rust and tawny, primeval and bare. South the land fell sharply into a valley along whose floor ran a road, and then rose again in fresh folds of hills. The nearest one was dominated by another large building which had been the Egyptian headquarters when the attack was on, further off a little town lay gently on the slopes. This was Bethlehem. Suddenly many things fell into place with an added dimension which was reality. Of course Bethlehem was an actual place, and it lay near to Jerusalem. To country folk travelling there, and in dire need of help and shelter it would be the obvious place to stop. And what more natural on these rolling hill-tops than that the shepherds should hear the angels sing. There was the road that went up to Jerusalem, only now there was a difference. This road no longer ran between Bethlehem and Jerusalem because a line of barbed wire cut across it, and on the other side of the hill a new road had been built by the Jordanians to connect once more the ancient city and the small town. Even the place where we stood bore

UNIVERSITY LECTURER

a name that was evocative, Rahel Ramat. In Rama, Rachel had wept for the children who had been massacred in the hope that one particular Baby might not survive.

That evening we were invited to a party to meet some of the Canadian and American staff from the Hebrew University. They lived near each other in a new suburb of plain rectangular houses arranged along the contours of the hillside. It was agreeable and interesting to be discussing Israeli ideas, for the first time in Israel, with those whose mother tongue was English, and they were not afraid to be critical where they felt criticism was due. There were three couples, all young, and all comparatively new Israeli citizens. When we rose to go an astonishing thing happened. As each couple said good night, passed over the doorstep and felt themselves to be alone, they changed the tongue in which they talked to each other from English into Hebrew. These men and women, from one of the least linguistically talented races, used as their private language a difficult foreign speech. There could have been no clearer indication of their passionate identification with this country. I remembered Deborah, whom we had met in Tel Aviv, telling us a story of the early days of the gathering-in. She herself was a middle-aged sabra who had seen the whole panorama of development and she described the struggle to create a nation out of so many disparate elements. A major factor in the situation was language, the total acceptance of this ancient Hebrew tongue and its revival as modern everyday speech by constant common use. The children, Deborah among them, went about the streets of Tel Aviv with pieces of paper on which were written, 'Hebrews speak Hebrew', and these they slipped into pockets of those whom they heard talking to each other in non-Hebrew speech. She would have felt here that the lesson had been well learnt.

109

'What do you do now?' I had asked Deborah. 'I teach our immigrants their own heroic history,' she replied. It seemed a fitting
corollary to her earlier activities.

We had been driven up to Jerusalem by Gershon, taking time he
could ill spare from his own work to enable us to see the maximum
of interest with the minimum of inconvenience or difficulty.

At first, as we left Tel Aviv, the country was flat, continously
covered with the spreading tentacles of a growing city. Gradually,
however, we left the town behind us and drove through rolling
agricultural acres where every now and again the tight circle of a
kibbutz or the rather more loose formation of a moshav set the seal
on possession of the land. We came to an inn at a point where the
road divided and the long-distance Jerusalem buses stopped for
passengers. Samson's Inn it was called.

'He was born round here,' said Gershon casually.

After this the road began to rise as we approached the escarpment.
In a shallow valley, whose floor was covered with stones, Gershon
said: 'That was where David fought Goliath,' as we whizzed by.

It was extraordinary to share a heritage like this with him, and I
am not sure that either of us liked it. We never referred to each
other's view of the Bible. 'Oh yes,' we said openly, maintaining as
detached an interest in an historical fact as he had himself, while we
looked at each other with eyes that expressed a great deal more. It
was here, actually here, that David, that legendary, sacred figure
of our own faith, had picked up a stone – the place was full of stones,
it was suddenly the obvious weapon after all instead of a faintly
childish substitute for arms – and killed the giant.

The road began to run into deep and narrow gorges. It twisted and
turned while on either side the rocks, planted with new forests or
supporting ancient olive trees, rose up above us to the slice of sky.
Every now and then, toppled mute and rusted in the ditch, lay the
burnt out corpse of a motor vehicle. At first we glanced at these
only out of the corners of our eyes. Good manners seemed to demand that we did not call attention to what could have been our
hosts' singular lack of road sense. Yet something did not quite ring
true in this explanation. Why so many wrecks? Why were all burnt
beyond any hope of reclamation? Why, more curious still, did some
have small wreaths of withered flowers or leaves hung on a distorted
radiator cap or laid gently on a contorted roof? We ventured a remark. Gershon focussed his eyes on a long-familiar sight.

'That was a food convoy going up to Jerusalem during the war. They were shot up from the air. We keep them to remind us. You know that Jerusalem is at the end of a corridor which is quite narrow, with Jordan close on both sides. To keep Jerusalem supplied was a major task. This was the only way, the only road, and they were under constant air attack. We lost many young men. We do not forget them.'

After that we could look openly at the relics, sometimes more than one locked together in a tangled heap. It was a vivid memorial. The harsh, sanguine metal had become part of the beautiful wild road, yet it was in no danger of merging imperceptibly into the land-scape. These were very modern monuments, serving as a reminder not only of the terrors and the dangers of war but also of the con-tinuing perils of the peace.

Now and again the hills would open on our left hand side and we would catch a glimpse, far away below us, of the flat coastal plain stretching to the sea. The veils of atmosphere spread over the land a soft blue haze which shifted and parted as the clouds sailed across the sun. Then, as abruptly as it had come, the view was gone and we were shut in again with the rising rocky hills. When we began to approach Jerusalem those hills took on an astonishing character. They remained forbidding, stony, unchanged in shape, but they were unremittingly cultivated from top to toe, in regular encircling lines of terracing. The levelled soil was supported by walls of stones, painstakingly and patiently collected, not over the years but over the centuries back into the dim mists of time. Here on these banded mountains, whose man-made stripes glowed honey and rust in the evening sun, the long labour of man to live and prosper was made visible. Some of the terraces were now unused, some had crumbled into decay, some were newly hewn and shaped; but new or old the method was the same. These stones had seen the ages come and go; those were the everlasting hills.

Gershon left us at the Hebrew University, itself newly hewn out of those same hills. A splendid complex of buildings, it stands high overlooking what is still essentially barrenness scored redly with the foundations of all the subsidiary housing which will grow up round it. The university is on a vast scale, proudly set on the edge of the hillside slope, so that on one side the structures overlook broad walks and terraced gardens, on the other hang directly above the valley like a fleet of ships alert to sail. Here the combination that has made Israel still marches hand in hand: learning and work. Financially most of the students are poor, seventy per cent are assisted by funds from government or other agencies, but many need as well to find work. The university makes special arrangements to cater for this difficulty, and even itself to employ as many students as possible, in laboratories, in libraries, as secretaries or even as guides, and classes are arranged to take place mainly in the afternoons to allow a job to be carried on in the mornings. These students are on the average older than students elsewere, because all must do their military service until the age of twenty or twenty-one. This means that a considerable number of them may be married, even have children and so the financial situation is still more complicated. But this is the reality of life in Israel and sensibly the university has adapted itself to it without any loss of function or dilution of results. The B.A. course lasts four years instead of three, to allow for the slower rate of progress of a working student, and there is no feeling of this being a place apart, an ivory tower of learning unrelated to the living world but rather the contrary. This is the power house which sets the pace.

The Hebrew University held one particular treasure that we very much wanted to see. Some of the Dead Sea Scrolls were on view, carefully set out and guarded and only visible if one were taken by an accredited guide. Our courier was a charming woman of middle age, cultured and accomplished, speaking perfect English. She accepted, with a half-concealed sigh at our obviousness I felt, that we wished to see the Scrolls, and she put it first on the tour, not only I think because it happened to be topographically convenient but also because she wished to have it out of the way so that we could concentrate on the real interest of the university.

We went down in a lift to an underground room where, in illuminated glass cases round the walls were displayed a fragment of Isaiah, a commentary on Habbakuk, and an ancient Book of Discipline. I do not quite know what I had expected to see, or to feel, or to be told. In the event it was the sight that was so astonishing. Here were no faded, tattered portions of parchment covered with indecipherable, spindly writing. No, these were strong, light, thick pages filled with open lines of vigorous dark calligraphy. They looked as if they might really have been written very recently; the ink was bold and brown, conveying directly a sense of the active hand and mind that had used it. As so often in Israel, the years

JERUSALEM STREET

dissolved and one was left with a revelation of the reality of history.
Was the excitement more for us because it was not only history but
something deeper and more far-reaching? I often wondered. For
our guide there was little interest in this visit, and when I asked her
some questions about the Scrolls and whether she could read them
she answered indifferently. Perhaps she had seen them too often,
and had always, anyway, accepted their reality. For us, our beliefs
eroded by scepticism and doubt, it seemed almost a miracle to see
even a minute portion of historic fact thus vitalised.

After that the magnificence of the university seemed common-
place. The superb lecture hall, the wonderful library, the great
courtyard filled with students of many nations, all these were of
our own day and age and their equivalent existed elsewhere. But it

was not often that one stood before a fragment from the remote past and felt it span the centuries with such instant, direct, human vigour.

The past and the present. Here in Jerusalem they were all the time intertwined: here no one tried to deny the past or shear it of its relevance. They could not do so, indeed, for at every turn the terraced hills bore witness to the generations of men who had tilled their soil, and the sacred city, though three times renewed, much fought for, many times overcome, still stood, a sign of the long continuity of man's relationship to God.

And man's relationship to man? The monuments in the new city bore witness to this also. Running along a great spur of hill, overlooking a rocky valley beyond which the heights marched rank on rank to the horizon, there was a new building. Low and blank and built of concrete, all its eyes turned inwards, it blended with the ridge yet retained an aspect of its own, unrelenting, faintly sinister. We did not visit it. Even the forbidding exterior seen across the valley as we returned from other ploys could cause us to shiver and fall silent. For this was the museum of remembrance where evidence was gathered of all that had happened to those peoples of the Jewish faith who had suffered and died in Europe in the twentieth century. Here, beyond any doubt, could be seen in photographs and documents and in the mute testimony of authentic relics the things that had been endured by men, women and children in concentration camps, in ghettos, on the streets, in cattle trucks and on the long slow marches which only led to death. For if these things were not, on the whole, remembered with great bitterness, neither were they forgotten. This too was part of the heritage and it was felt right that the generations to come should also know what their people had endured.

I say we did not go. We felt we could not face it. Maybe the meetings which we had had with the living representatives of this holocaust had already haunted our dreams and stirred our imaginations so that we felt we could not contemplate the horrors any more. But the museum was not the only place of remembrance and one other we did see. This was on Mount Zion.

Mount Zion lies on the same side of the valley as the old city, on the same hilltop to the south of the city wall. It has remained in Jewish hands, and the border creeps all round it in a tangle of barbed wire and broken masonry and odd shell holes, so that one is always conscious of its being not only a hallowed place but also a battle ground.

This, the holy mountain, is the only ancient sacred place left in Israeli hands, and as such it has begun to attract the legend-makers in a way it never did before. Here one can almost see myths being created for future generations. Mount Zion holds a complex of buildings belonging to both Jewish and Christian faiths. It is topped by a huge church, whose dome is bullet-pitted, the cupola above it packed with sandbags. They will show you the room where the l ast Supper was said to have taken place, but in its bare shabby emptiness all atmosphere or authenticity has long ago been swept away. On the lower slopes, huge, barren and desolate, a building gazes back over the valley to the Scottish church of St Andrew riding proudly on the other side. Over the door a shabby notice still says: Church Missionary Society, but in the back yard the mortars have made great pits in the ground and there is an eerie air of ambush in the quietness. Up the steep stone steps to the next terrace, passed by nuns' and priests and chattering tourists, we emerged on to a flat space where it seemed that bad commercialism had taken over. Notices pointed to a shop, filled with cheap souvenirs and gaudy picture postcards. All the most sacred symbols of both Jew and Christian were hawked for gain to those who passed by. Notices in Hebrew and in Roman characters pointed to the holy places, though it seemed indeed that only these notices which referred to Jewish sacred spots were translated for the benefit of visitors into the Roman alphabet, and if there were instructions how to get to the Christian points of pilgrimage they were left discreetly uninterpreted.

For both, however, King David's tomb seemed to be an essential shrine to visit and so we wound our way through gardens and echoing stone caverns of halls until we found ourselves in a small room with an ancient bearded rabbi sitting ruminating in one corner. With a little crowd we pushed through yet another door into an even smaller room where, fenced off against one wall, there was something covered with a cloth and decorated with tatty gilt and silver offerings. Behind the railing a rabbi, white-coated like a rather seedy grocer, greeted us and prepared to put up a prayer for those of any faith, Christian, Moslem, Jew. Beside us a nun made a faint gesture of distaste and turned away; her companion, a huge cheerful-looking priest turned his back too. I sympathised with them—till I saw that underneath his cassock the priest was fiddling with the stops of a magnificent cine camera!

The purveyor of the tomb, meanwhile, had whipped back the cloth and revealed a blackened stone of undoubted antiquity. With engaging honesty he then admitted that it was doubtful whether this was King David's tomb, but it might be, and he implied that we had better all be on the safe side. In a little room beyond the old man had begun to wail, lost in his own mystery. We passed on repelled, but unmoved. And yet, and yet. Everywhere man's human nature struggles daily with his spiritual self, and it is when the things he holds most sacred are no longer part of the common turmoil of his life that they cease to have the truth of reality for him. David had told us of a Scottish doctor whom he had taken on this same pilgrimage. He had expected a reaction such as ours of distaste and disbelief. But the doctor had stood gravely, gazing on all the tawdry trappings that concealed the tomb, and then he had said: 'Is it not wonderful. This man's poetry will be sung over my grave,' and with courteous thanks he turned away. The deeps and shallows of our lives run side by side. We should accept it when they intermingle and not cast ourselves aside on an indifferent shore.

We left King David's tomb and followed the notices which said: To the Chamber of Destruction. We did not know what we were going to see, it just seemed a pity not to see it all when we were there. Then suddenly, down some steps into what looked and felt like an underground cave, reality burst upon us. Round the walls row upon row of plaques, some large, some small, commemorated those villages which had been destroyed all over Europe and listed numbers of their inhabitants who had perished. They were written in Hebrew, but in each case the name of the village stood out clear and the numbers of the dead. Village after village, camp after camp, the figures varying but always terrible. Hundreds here, thousands there. Six million dead, remembered not individually but in their communities in this place. The candles sputtered uncertainly; an old man keened constantly in prayer. It was a sound appropriate to the place and what it stood for. The loud voices of a group of sightseers who had followed us in seemed an affront to the spirits remembered here. One longed to quiet them lest they should rouse some terrible revenge.

Let into the walls were cavities, glass-fronted, and here there were displayed a few things which recalled the mind from impersonal horror of unbelievable figures to the personal terror of those who had composed them. Soap and ashes, both from human bodies; the parchment, for God knows what uses, which was a human skin; the Jewish books, brought out concealed in shoes and bags, or sewn up into shirts, and all, all steeped in blood.

It was astonishing to come out and down again into the cheerfulness and bustle of the new Jerusalem. The revealed depth of man's inhumanity to man seemed in some measure to be counterbalanced by astonishment at the resilience, the courage and the endurance of the human spirit. There was another memorial to the human spirit, but this time of quite a different kind. Set in gardens on a quiet hill, its calm and civilised peace totally at variance with the battle-scarred holiness of Mount Zion, was the tomb of Theodore Herzl, the father of the State of Israel. It was Herzl, an Austro-Hungarian Jew, who in the latter half of the nineteenth century had had a vision of a Jewish home, and had fought and planned for it, negotiating with diplomats who might help him to further this dream, inspiring and being inspired by those of his own people in Eastern Europe who perceived as he did that the long Jewish exile might be drawing to its close. It was to Herzl that the offer was made by the British Government of a grant of land in Uganda, an offer which he was at one time inclined to accept but which his fellow Jews rejected utterly as not being the Promised Land. What would now have been the position of the Jewish State had it been accepted? It was Herzl who set the sights and started the movement whose momentum was eventually, after much hardship, to sweep Israel into existence.

With all this in our minds it was astonishing to see in the small museum which held his papers and photographs, the complete reconstruction of his study, tables, chairs, pens, books, etc., all lovingly transported from Europe, and many historic and interesting documents, a picture of a middle-aged man in a full, dark beard. This was no frail old prophet, grown white in the struggle to make a dream come true, this was a man in the full vigour and prime of his life who had died in 1904 at the age of forty-four. He never saw the country he lived and died for; for him Israel remained a promise and a dream; but the words which drove him forward are repeated here: 'Wenn Ihr es wollt, ist es kein märchen; If you will it, it is no longer a fairy tale.' When the time came that the dream took on reality and life Herzl's body was brought in honour to the land which owed so much to him. Now it lay under a flat stone slab beneath a vast sky, with the Jerusalem hills standing guard around it, while children ran about the paths between the flower beds not understanding what made their parents talk with lowered voices and tread with lighter and more silent steps.

Jerusalem held for us one contemporary interest. Working there were two young British volunteers from Voluntary Service Overseas, and having started this organisation ourselves in 1958 we were naturally interested in how it had developed. Tudor and Helena, both aged eighteen, were in projects which were the concern of the Social Welfare Department.

In some ways it was curious to find British volunteers here at all. Israel is a country which is trying to find its own outlets overseas for the skills of its people; it is concerned to enlarge its scope as a giving country rather than a receiving one. For when it comes to receiving it has, after all, a continuing stream of new immigrants, a young indigenous generation which is still active and idealistic, and the enormous and vital financial help of world Jewry. Where then could it be said with any honesty that two young people from Britain, neither of them with Jewish backgrounds, were needed to give help of any importance?

The answer was an interesting one, for it pin-pointed a malaise which was by no means unique to Israel. The desperate shortage of staff in social welfare institutions and of teachers in schools. It was true that these positions were poorly paid, but inadequate salary does not wholly account for the tendency in many countries, including our own, to leave the care of the ailing and the handicapped increasingly to those from outside the community. It was into this situation, the one in a village for mentally handicapped children, the other in an orthopaedic hospital, that Tudor and Helena had a contribution to make. Physical pioneering was a rapidly shrinking field for young Israelis, but sociological pioneering had barely begun and its challenge was enormous. In Britain as well as in Israel the job was to open up opportunities in this area to young people and to prove their ability to rise to them.

There is in Israel a professional touchiness in relation to those from outside which warns the stranger and the visitor to walk warily and talk with care. It is the natural sensitivity of a new nation which fears patronage, perhaps augmented in this case by certain special factors. The Israeli population began by being unique in that where in other countries the intellectuals were the top of a pyramid whose broad base was composed of those who worked with their hands for a living, the Israeli population pyramid stood the other way up; the purely manual worker being a tiny percentage compared to the large numbers of intellectuals. But rapid immigration from Asian and North African countries has begun to alter this picture, and there is some fear too that it may begin to affect the standards which the new nation set itself. It is one thing to have a population which is highly literate and uses its literacy for cerebral pleasure, it is another to find yourself coping with an influx of adult illiterates who have no background of learning from books. It may be that those with professional qualifications, who had been accustomed to a national climate where even the most humble had an intellectual background, have become sensitive to the possibility that there could be an increasing gap between the top of the pyramid and its middle echelons who necessarily compose a high percentage of staff in social welfare institutions. We were told of a number of British nurses who had been asked to come out for a limited period to help train their counterparts in Israeli hospitals. Few survived the time envisaged, and this seemed astonishing. The reasons were simple to find, though they may have been complex to deal with. Because of professional sensitivity and jealousy the British nurses were not allowed to do anything except the most humble and menial jobs in the wards. It was not felt right that they should take any kind of precedence over an Israeli nurse, whatever her qualifications. In those circumstances any real idea of helping with training became absurd, and gradually the British nurses, each in her own way highly qualified, decided that this was time-wasting and left. It may be that this was an extreme case, though the Israeli who described it to us did not seem to think so, but it does illustrate a genuine difficulty when it comes to the offering of help.

Tudor and Helena, however, started with a great advantage. They had no qualifications at all and somehow this, which might have been an affront, made them acceptable. Helena, especially, was given work to do which carried great responsibility, but her youth and her obvious acceptance of any role which was required of her robbed this fact of its sting. It may be that the British nurses too brought with them their own share of professional pride and that this was the one thing needed to close the doors utterly against them.

We first met Tudor the afternoon before the start of the Sabbath, which begins at sundown on Friday and ends at sundown on Saturday.

He was working at a village for seriously mentally handicapped children, Kfar Hashvedi, just outside Jerusalem, where his job was to be a general handyman and to help with projects and games. It was not wholly satisfactory, for much of what he might have been able to do was handicapped by his lack of Hebrew and the low grade of mental deficiency of the children. He did not know we were coming, indeed he did not know us at all, and as we drove off the main road and down through the gate I wondered what sort of young man we should find.

Our car stopped, and David went into the office to try to discover where in this warren of buildings we should find a young man from Britain. He came out with some complicated directions and we began to move towards the house indicated. On the way we passed one of the 'children', a large, shambling young man very obviously mentally handicapped. My husband stopped and said the name we wanted several times very clearly:

'Tudor. Tudor.'

The boy looked at us without comprehension, though with a friendly, dog-like gaze.

'Tudor,' we said again.

Suddenly something happened. Slowly the name began to assume a shape and a meaning in his mind.

'Yudor,' he said. 'Yudor,' and seeing our pleased assent he came up confidently and began to pull us forward, round the back of a small row of rooms to a door. 'Yudor,' he shouted, 'Yudor,' and he banged happily and with assurance on the wooden panel. Before we had ever seen him this told us something about the young man we were going to meet.

Tudor came to the door in answer to the hammering and was covered in embarrassment to find three strange adults standing outside, but he asked us in and hastily cleared the bed, where he had been lying reading the Old Testament, to give us somewhere to sit. He was a tall, young man with a gentle, open smile. He had taken some trouble to prepare himself for this assignment, even going to visit the rabbi in his home town in England to try to gain some knowledge of Jewish thought and custom. This proved to have been time well spent, for now that he was here he found himself working in an institution which was rigidly orthodox in its religious observance, and this was no easy position for a young foreigner unless he had a sincerely religious purpose of his own and some

small understanding of Jewish Law. Tudor had both. It was interesting to find that social welfare came under the wing of the religious party in Parliament, which meant that most institutions were orthodox—in contrast to the sociologists who were, on the whole, openly agnostic.

He took us out immediately to show us something of the village and its surroundings before the Sabbath actually started and it became difficult to do so. David had left us and we wandered out to the edge of the village which is hung, as was so often the case in Jerusalem, over the edge of the hill. Away beneath us, already in the evening shadow, a small town spread itself over the lower slopes. It had a curiously European air, its principal landmarks being churches and the cypress-dark enclosed gardens of monasteries. This was Ein Carem, where John the Baptist was born and Mary came to meet his mother Elizabeth. Its golden stones glowing in a gathering golden dusk backed by the ancient terraces, with an air both mediaeval and archaic about its small stone houses, one had no difficulty in seeing it as the scene of this encounter. Tudor pointed out the various monasteries to us and described their present-day predicaments. The huge Italian monastery, now with only two men in it, who feared to let this depletion of their numbers be generally known in case they were attacked. By who? By the village perhaps, divided in its heritage. The Russian and Greek Orthodox communities who bred pigs secretly in this land where the pig was an animal unclean. But from above none of these conflicts and divergencies could shatter the quiet, timeless calm of the steadily approaching Sabbath.

That was the old world. When we raised our eyes higher there, supported on a saddleback between two lines of hills, riding like a great ship about to set sail into the sea of night, stood the Hadassah Hospital, two tall semi-circular towers joined by a forbidding great block and lightened by rows and rows of windows. As we gazed at it a puff of smoke rose up into the clear air from a gigantic pipe at one side, and, like a signal, the lights began, one by one, to go on all over that enormous vessel. Here the work of healing went on day and night, and while the Sabbath was observed in the little synagogue with the lovely windows by Chagall, it did not bring to a standstill, as it did in Kfar Hashvedi, much of the ordinary interchange of daily life.

For now the moon had come up behind us. A great yellow circle in an ash-grey, darkening sky. Along the horizon the new surburbs stretched their rows of rectangular houses, white and pink and orange among the eternal golden rocks, and in front of them, huge and dark against the moon, loomed over us the boy who had taken us to Tudor's door, murmuring 'Yudor. Yudor.'

'He's a very good footballer, you know,' said Tudor, with affection and some surprise in his voice.

There were no lights in the village, for Sabbath had begun and only candle light was permitted, nor was writing allowed among the strictly religious. In a hotel in Haifa we had seen a notice in the lounge which said: 'Guests will please refrain from writing on the Sabbath', and here, in Kfar Hashvedi, this prohibition was also maintained. As a matter of fact Tudor was homeless over the Sabbath, because his room belonged, in reality, to two girls who returned to occupy it for the weekends. During that period he lived in the little dispensary, sleeping on a high, cold, medical bed. Now, when we spoke of taking him back with us into Jerusalem for an evening meal he said, in some surprise at our ignorance:

'But there will be no buses running. They all stop when the Sabbath starts.'

We were disconcerted by this. The centre of Jerusalem was some miles away, easy enough in a motor car but a considerable distance to walk at night, even if we had known the way.

'Can we phone for a taxi?' we asked, feeling alien by now in the quiet, shuttered village.

Tudor's voice held some doubt: 'We're not supposed to use the telephone on the Sabbath. It is forbidden. And I don't know whether we could find a taxi that would agree to come now that Sabbath has started.' Then, perhaps seeing our downcast faces, he spoke more cheerfully. 'I'll try. Wait here and I'll see if I can't use the telephone without anyone knowing.'

He was not gone very long before he returned, smiling to himself.

'It's all right. I've found a taxi and he's coming straight away, but we must go down to the gate to wait for him because he won't be allowed to drive in on the Sabbath. It isn't permitted here to ride in a vehicle.'

It was full dark, though still with a splendid yellow moon hung above us in the sky, while we stood just behind the forbidding wire gate waiting for the lights of the taxi to come along the road. The watchman looked at us disapprovingly, or so we imagined, such was the atmosphere of religious observance generated in the village. At one and the same time we were shut in and also shut out, and we looked for signs of the taxi almost like refugees gazing out across a frontier for any hope of rescue. When it came, purring quietly, looking perfectly normal, we climbed in with a sense of relief. It was a relief undisturbed by any anxieties about financial disagreements with the taxi driver, for tipping is unknown in Israel. It is not until one actually experiences this state of affairs that one realises how fraught with difficulties life is for the stranger in countries where this custom does not pertain, and conversely how pleasureable life is when services are rendered without constant pressure for an added bonus to the agreed remuneration.

After that we saw a good deal of Tudor, quietly stuffing him with enormous meals and with some extra stimulus in the way of ideas. We had visited some of his patients in the village and had been saddened by their terrible condition and the impersonal handling of the hard-pressed staff. Here, as much as anywhere else in the world, there was a crying need for those who could give both love and time to the sore afflicted.

Then we met Helena. Helena was eighteen and she hoped eventually to train as a doctor. She worked in an orthopaedic hospital for crippled children. She was a girl of resource and efficiency who during the three months she had been in Israel had taught herself sufficient Hebrew to be able to carry on independent conversation with those she met. This was as well, for she was occasionally faced with situations which disconcerted her because the alive, modern character of Israel made them unexpected. Such was the day when she was stopped by the Jerusalem police while she was driving the hospital ambulance through the streets. At first she could not understand why this had happened. They asked for her licence and examined her papers, but they did not seem really interested in them. Most of all, openly, they examined her. She came eventually to the conclusion that they were surprised and rather put out to see a woman driving an ambulance. But why should this be in a country where the women do their military service alongside the men? The mystery was never resolved.

We visited Helena's hospital, taking Tudor with us. It was old, shabby, inconvenient and ramshackle, though beautifully equipped through the generosity of an American women's group. The staff were simple, mostly from oriental backgrounds, and with the exception of the sister-in-charge they had very little training. Just as in Britain, hospitals are forced to find a high percentage of their staff from among foreign applicants, so in Israel they are dependent for much of their labour force in social welfare institutions on low-grade oriental immigrants. Helena herself had been given full authority over a ward very soon after she arrived, and her natural friendliness and obvious willingness to undertake any kind of work had somehow made this arrangement acceptable to all the indigenous staff. Helena had felt, from her observations of the first few weeks, that there was one aspect of the care that she would like to alter. This was the matter of punishment. The staff shortage was so acute that a fairly rigorous system of punishment was used to keep the children in order and well disciplined. When Helena was asked if she would take over a ward of twenty-four children with four nurses under her, she made one stipulation. This was that she should be allowed to drop the punishment system and run things her own way. Matron, who was a very nice woman, agreed but with the warning that this would probably mean riotous behaviour in her ward and that she must be prepared to cope with it herself. So they waited to see what happened. Nothing happened, except that Helena became much beloved by her children.

We had an opportunity of seeing this for ourselves the day we went to visit the hospital with her. No sooner had the taxi debouched us at the door than there were cries coming from all sides. 'Helena, Helena,' small, chirrupy voices called out, and the strangest little human beings hobbled and hopped and crawled around us. They were, many of them, desperately crippled, some lying strapped immovable in their great beds, others getting themselves around with extraordinary agility considering the contraptions of leather and iron and wood they had perforce to carry with them. One wondered how it had ever been thought necessary to institute a punishment system at all. But whatever the reasons for this, the atmosphere was one of warmth and friendliness. There was no clinical detachment here, for many of the children it cannot have differed so very much from their homes, with the same rapid shifts from family loving to family chiding. There may not have been the highest standards of meticulous hygenic care, but we could not help wondering whether for the children the more normal atmosphere of mild squalor might not in the end be equally beneficial.

Helena had at one point managed to get hold of, quite how we never knew, a motor scooter. On this she had given rides, to their enormous excitement and pleasure, to those who were capable of moving about and who could manage to sit on a pillion seat. She had had races on improvised go-carts down the wide pitted drive under the cypress trees. She had piled some into the back of a van and taken them on little expeditions. She had brought with her a warmth, a willingness to experiment and a real love of children which was welcomed by everyone in the hospital; for unless the staff had responded with a warmth of their own she would not have been able to do much that she actually did. But I wonder if the real thing that she brought with her was not simply this, a heightened sense of living and loving which came from the knowledge that someone from outside the familiar circle cared enough to come and help.

It is in the ability to use a young volunteer that art lies. The realisation that what has arrived on the doorstep is not just a gap-filler, not one more helper to do the same things that were done yesterday and will be done again tomorrow, is not yet given to very many. For the young volunteer, precisely because he or she is young, brings with him a new dimension, an opportunity not simply to get more work done but to do creatively many things that have up till now been left undone. As we grow older it is, paradoxically, fear that inhibits us from fulfilling the dreams that we had when we were young. We may have lost the fears of our childhood, but we have gained new ones: fear of change, particularly when it may affect our own established way of living; fear of non-conformity, which may make us different among those whom we have chosen to be our friends; fear of involvement, which may split open our cosy family circle. But the young, on the threshold of adulthood, do not share these fears, or if they do they see them still as something to be overcome. For them change, which is their natural climate at this time, is to be welcomed. They long to be different and individual, even when they are at their most conformist. They need and want to be involved in the life of their community as a whole rather than in a small restricted group. These are assets which contain dynamism, and any institution which has at its command a supply of young volunteers has also infinite possibilities of creative expansion and exploration. But this is a challenge to the whole of society and adult wisdom and imagination are also needed so that fresh opportunities may be constantly opening up before the younger generation.

On the Saturday, which was of course the Sabbath, Tudor had breakfast with us in our hotel and then we all went out to walk about and absorb the sight of the streets of Jerusalem. It was a lovely morning in early December. The air was fresh and clear, the sky blue and a sparkling sun shone on the honey-coloured houses, the red-tiled roofs and the dark evergreen trees which flung pools of shade into the enclosed gardens. At the busy intersection, where the roads met momentarily on the level before plunging once again up or down hills, porters usually lounged waiting for work. Except for the padded protector hung over his back to soften the harshness of his burdens, the tallest of these might have been an English squire, plus-fours, tweed jacket, large dark moustache, topped by a knitted woollen cap. At their corner we turned up a side street and struck away from the commercial centre of the town towards the border.

Presently we began to enter a more ancient quarter, where the houses had a closed blank look and the silence was undisturbed by any vehicle or by the careless chatter of ordinary city crowds. The people we did see were increasingly strange to us, and we began to feel more and more conspicuous. Our own voices dropped to whispers and I quietly returned my sketchbook and pencil, which I had been carrying in my hand, back to the safe concealment of my handbag. It was the Sabbath, and this was the Mea She'arim, the religious quarter of Jerusalem.

The people who lived here had come from Eastern Europe long before the establishment of the state of Israel, in order to await the coming of the Messiah in the Holy Land. They were fanatically religious and for them there was no such thing as twentieth-century change and development. They lived, as they had always lived, by the Torah and the Talmud. Mea She'arim, the Hundred Gates quarter, was so called because it used once to be surrounded by a high wall and many gates, separating it from the fallen and frivolous life outside. The walls and the gates had long ago crumbled into oblivion, or been pulled down,

JERUSALEM PORTER

but Mea She'arim retained its isolation by means of a fierce religious prejudice. These were the Chosen People, and they had no doubt about it.

Walking gravely past us in the streets were men and boys on their way to worship in the many synagogues. They might have walked out of old Polish or Hungarian pictures, so extraordinary was their dress. Pale, bearded faces looked through us from under huge circular fur hats. Over their shoulders, above long black robes, hung white shawls with striped borders. Young men, long corkscrew ringlets hanging down in front of their ears under wide, flat black hats, hurried by their spindly legs protruding from under straight black coats. Small boys, grave and solemn, walked beside their grandfathers, their blond hair trained too in corkscrew curls beneath their round cloth skull caps. A long, light, open coat covered a loose white robe. Later, on the very edge of the quarter, we came across a band of these little boys kicking a ball about as all boys do, their ordinary occupation contrasting curiously with their tossing curls and air of having missed a century or two. What happened when they went to school, we wondered, and then remembered this was Israel where the welding together of widely different elements was recognised as a vital national purpose.

We had begun to feel at the same time invisible and all too recognisable. We were beneath contempt, but we were well aware that we might also be an affront, when, suddenly, a huge notice slung across the street proclaimed in three languages: 'Jewish daughter, the Torah obligates you to dress with modesty. We do not tolerate people passing through our streets immodestly dressed!' I became only too aware that what I considered ordinary apparel might appear indecent to men accustomed to full-length skirts and high-necked long-sleeved garments on their women. I was glad now that the sketchbook was out of sight. It might well have been construed as a flagrant breach of the Sabbath, making a graven image and, in a sense, a form of writing.

These people, who are a tiny minority in the population of Israel, could nevertheless be a grave embarrassment to her, for they do not recognise the secular Israeli state. Indeed they had gone so far at one point as to march over the border with a white flag in order to surrender to the Arabs, saying that it was the destiny of the Jewish people to live under a foreign conqueror. The Arabs did not understand their scruples and sent them back, but it is no easy

thing for a nation as small as Israel to contain a fanatical minority. They do not speak Hebrew, but use Yiddish for their everyday tongue, saying that Hebrew is the sacred language and not for common use. It is kept for the synagogue, and for the day when the Messiah will come. It was a sect within a sect from the Mea She'arim, who felt that it was not enough that they should keep the Sabbath strictly but that they had a mission to make others do the same, who caused damaging riots some time before we had arrived by stoning and overturning any vehicles which ventured near the borders of their quarter and setting fire to them. All this could have been merely an exasperation to the body politic, but it was more than that. Israel is poised still upon the pinnacle of decision between Israeli nationality and Jewish religion. The old question of race and faith has not yet been publicly resolved, with each agreeing to play their part in a common whole. In the welter of Israeli politics the minority religious party is important in a balance of power, and to that minority religious party the people of the Mea She'arim, while dissociating themselves from secular concerns, are an embarrassment.

We strolled self-consciously on, down the silent streets where balconied and shuttered windows excluded us. From the synagogues the strange, wailing services went on and on. Our curiosity was smothered by solemnity, and it was with something of relief that we eventually arrived at the bounds of the Hundred Gates and found ourselves in the freer air beyond. We were not far from the Mandelbaum Gate, the only point of contact left in the whole length of the Arab–Israeli border; of official contact that is. Even at the Mandelbaum Gate that contact is devious and concealed.

The Arab checkpoint lay not directly in front of us but to our right, over a rise and round a corner. The term Gate, with its straightforward connotations, was misleading. Just for a moment the desire to see whether forbidden fruit could not, after all, be plucked overcame us. My husband had his passport on him and he took it out of his pocket and advanced towards the Israeli guard. He did not get far. With courtesy, but with a firmness there was no mistaking, he was told that in order to cross he must have a special paper provided by our Embassy. Tudor was talking, I remember, about the behaviour of humanity in a

ORTHODOX MAN

nuclear war and his depression at the thought of it. I looked at the tangled barbed wire which stretched away in front of us and wondered whether a more profitable speculation might not be to scrutinize our own behaviour here and now.

ORTHODOX BOY

CHAPTER VII

Nothing New under the Sun

HILAL

HILAL stepped over the sill of the low, open windows of our Tel
Aviv hotel and greeted us with a broad grin and a cheerful 'shalom'.
In his expression as he looked at us there was a faintly speculative
element; this dramatically carefree entrance was meant to indicate
something to us and he wondered whether we were friendly enough
and perceptive enough to gather what it was. Hilal was never
absolutely certain whose side we were on. His essentially simple
and charming nature was ready to take us on trust as friends,
but every now and then his sabra's pride put out its antennae
fearful of detecting denigration or indifference in our attitude. His
entrance through the window, which delighted us with its jaunty
flamboyance, was intended to remind us daily that Israel was a
country of informality and equality, and Israelis people who did
what they felt like without fear of social solecism.

Hilal was a mixed-up kid. He was a large, strong, young man with
deep-set, clear eyes in a broad high-cheeked face topped by close-

132

cropped hair. He was one of the youngest members of the Ministry of Agriculture's Foreign Training Department, and as our stay progressed he was allocated more and more frequently to be our guide. His English was very good; he had been twice in Britain studying but told us rather plaintively that he had not enjoyed it.

'Why not?' we asked, disappointed that this attractive young Israeli should have found us wanting.

'I was homesick,' he answered simply.

He loved his country passionately and with an almost old-fashioned fervour, deploring that his own contemporaries, as he felt, lacked this same feeling. He was profoundly idealistic, and enjoyed telling us long and often involved parables to illustrate his points about the state of life, love and the world. Sometimes he would fear that we were laughing at him and his manner would sharpen and a moody frown darken his brow, while he glanced at us suspiciously out of one corner of an eye and pressed his foot on the accelerator to drive a little faster. He did not understand our jokes at all, and often we could see that he was searching to find where the point was meant to prick his own armour. He need not have feared. We liked and admired him and while we may occasionally have smiled at each other when he struggled to be articulate about the problems that beset him and his generation it was always with affection and never with malice.

Like so many young Israelis whose jobs placed them in the urban environment of cities, as government officials, in commerce or in law, Hilal's home was in a moshav; in his case it was a well-known moshav which had been one of the early pioneers of this form of settlement, Kfar Vitkin. One day, when he had finally assured himself that we were trustworthy and genuine, he asked us to go home with him and have an evening meal with his father and mother. We accepted gladly. We knew by now that it was a sign of real respect to be invited into an Israeli home.

Kfar Vitkin had long lost the outward signs of its pioneering past. The trees had flourished, the crops were lush, the houses had the established appearance of buildings which have grown to belong to the land they stand on. As always the house was very simple inside, clean and bare but with the essential convenience of electricity, running water and refrigerator. It required a very great effort of imagination to visualise this place as the swamp it had been thirty-three years before when Hilal's parents arrived from Europe.

MEXICAN STUDENT

Then life had been one constant, unremitting struggle, not only with the land but with disease also. Every three weeks some member of the family had been struck down with malaria.

Neither of the parents spoke any English, but there was no doubt about the warmth of their welcome. This was a working family on an active farm, and when we arrived there were still the cows to milk and the chickens in their muttering thousands to be shut up for the night. Hilal immediately changed into huge farm boots and went out to the barn with his father to help, taking my husband with him. I smiled at the mother and attempted to make some kind of communication while I watched her prepare the simple meal of cheese and bread and fruit. We ate it presently in a relaxed and comfortable atmosphere without restraints or inhibitions.

It is Israel's strength that she still has a large number of young men who can move, as Hilal did, from the sophistication of the town to the simplicity of the small country farm without feeling estrangement or inferiority. In the training she can offer to young men of other countries overseas this equilibrium between town and country is one of her major assets.

Israel is fortunate in that she has no money to dispose of to anyone overseas. So she is saved from the misconstructions, the greed, the pride, the competition that seems inevitably to surround any financial transaction. She has only her own people and her skills, and on these terms she is acceptable to many new nations in Africa and Asia. She has another great advantage. She is a developing country herself yet, by unique circumstances, she has at the same time all the technological know-how of much older and more settled communities. Her skills are of a high order, but her problems are still the basic problems of any new nation. She has had to make a bare land blossom, and it is still possible to see clearly in Israel highly instructive lessons set out visually of how this was done: 'before' and 'after' can be observed in the same day, sometimes in the same glance. She has had to cope, is indeed coping, with the resettlement of populations, with large-scale adult illiteracy, with the problems of forming one nation from many different elements. All this experience can be invaluable to other developing territories, and, because Israel too is a small country struggling to find her own identity, they feel able to accept it.

Israel needs to have outlets for giving. She has been at the receiving end of a constant stream of immigrants and of financial aid from world Jewry, but it is not until she too can see herself in the position of giving assistance that she can really believe in her own nationhood and independence. There are simpler reasons too. Isolated on the edge of a seaboard with enemies all around and at her back, she needs friends, and she would be the first to admit that her overseas aid may help to fulfil this purpose. She is right to admit this. We are never wholly trusted when we say that our motives are purely altruistic, and it does not detract from the aid in the eyes of other countries if they know that their help also is being sought in return.

There were two ways of imparting knowledge and skill to others. The first was to send overseas Israeli instructors to live and work among the local people in whatever country they were needed to adapt their own experience to local conditions and use their own background of unafraid experimentation to bring new ideas and fresh thinking into age-old ways of working the land. The second way was to bring over to Israel from Africa and Asia

YOUNG ETHIOPIAN

certain key young men and to open their eyes and their minds to the possibilities of twentieth-century agriculture. Our friend Gershon was in charge of the second aspect of the Ministry of Agriculture's Foreign Training Department's programme.

Gershon was himself a very remarkable man, and he saw the role of his department in an unusual light, and one that was not always entirely acceptable to his colleagues. He believed that what his courses were trying to do was not so much to inculcate agricultural knowledge as to change or to create an attitude of mind. Contrary to appearances he felt that what Israel had to offer to the young man who came to her shores for an agricultural training was not primarily specialised knowledge of what crops to grow and how, or where to acquire the latest in mechanised implements and how to use them; nor was it necessarily to learn how to house new village communities and organise their local government. All these activities had Israeli features which were not transferable, and some depended on an amount of financial aid which would be impossible in an African or Asian setting.

'No,' said Gershon, 'Our contribution is quite different. The gospel is WORK. What we can show them is how to work. We don't give them the solutions. But we can show them how to solve problems. And we can show them that a man need not be ashamed to be educated and to be a small farmer. It is an attitude we want to try to change. An attitude which says that farming can be conducted from an office: that it is beneath the dignity of a man of standing to work with his hands in the fields: that it is only large and expensive ideas which are worth having. All this we can try to change. Technical knowledge is easy to get. Many countries already have first-class research stations and agricultural colleges. It is not that that holds back progress, rather it is the inability, or the unwillingness, of those who know to communicate their knowledge to those who don't know. They won't take themselves out of their research stations and their laboratories to work alongside the man whose life is spent in the fields. We can help here: we can show them how to work.'

This emphasis on an attitude had led Gershon to a second important proviso. The courses must be short. A young man who came to Israel must not stay so long there that he began to feel the pull of more sophisticated societies than his own. He must return to his own country while the revelation of what he had learnt still burned within him, and while his home and his country still called clearly to him. With too long a stay the ties weakened and the attraction of yet more education, or of a little further travel, grew stronger and stronger. This meant a training which was counted in months rather than in years, so that the intensity could be retained right through it. For Mr C., who was concerned with the fields rather than the minds of men, this was a hard doctrine to accept, going, as it did, against the slow, ordered rhythm of seedtime and harvest. But for Gershon it was cardinal, and our own experience in West Africa bore him out.

The course then was so arranged that the young man who arrived found himself not, as he had perhaps hoped, sitting in classrooms in college imbibing knowledge but a participant fully integrated into the ordinary daily work of Israeli agriculture. There was formal instruction, but it was sandwiched between spells of hard work, and both contributed to the whole and were essential to it. So that the Ghanaian or the Ugandan coming to Israel would have a short period of orientation and would then find himself, clad in jeans and a blue stitched hat, immersed in the day to day work of a kibbutz or a moshav. After five or six weeks, aware now what the real problems were in terms of people and of land, he might find himself back in an agricultural college gaining some of the theory to help solve the difficulties. And in a few weeks more he would be out again sharing the troubles and triumphs of yet another form of communal settlement. He was never an observer, an interested looker-on, viewing Israeli life. He was in it from the beginning, part of it, carrying his share.

It seemed a fairly simple proposition to the Israelis in the early days. 'We, too, have suffered,' they said. 'We have been oppressed. We know what it is to be sensitive about our own national self-esteem. We are a young and struggling nation too, and our hands are extended to our brothers.' They looked at the British, floundering amid the treacherous waters of nationalism and independence in many of the overseas territories, with interracial conflict and a general tendency on the part of the rest of the world to denigrate her contribution to development, and the Israelis smiled a little, as a young man will smile at an older one whose best he feels has not been good enough. 'Now,' they said. 'We will show you how it can be done.'

This was in the early days. They are wiser and sadder now, and more aware that some of the problems which afflict us are common human problems deep in the nature of man.

'It is not so easy as we thought,' said one of our guides with a wry smile.

A major problem was one which has always beset many kinds of overseas training. Was the man who was chosen to come for it necessarily the same man who was going to be most useful back in his own country? Many of the Foreign Training Department's agricultural students were government servants in their own lands, some were even ex-ministers, and as such their main interest was not to go back in order to become a farmer but to use the prestige of an overseas course to further a career in administration or politics, either local or national. They felt themselves to be coming to Israel as ambassadors, to observe and to discuss in formal classes. Very few of them had ever worked with their hands and they had a deep-seated resistance to so doing. It was all right in Israel, where they were away from their own people and outside their own traditions, but they knew well what would be expected of them when they went back and the strength that would be needed if they were to stand out against the pressure of public opinion in their own countries. The task was not impossible, but it was considerably more difficult than it had seemed in the early days when the Israelis had felt that a really good example at last would go a long way towards solving the problems.

There were other shocks in store. The communal settlements, the kibbutzim, which to like-minded Israelis had an easily understandable philosophy, however many practical difficulties there might be to resolve, were not so simply explained to an African, sometimes just because he was prepared to accept its basic premises completely. One young Tanganyikan, who had greatly enjoyed his experience in a kibbutz, wrote some months later from Africa to say that he was sending his young son back to his kibbutz to be educated by them. When they had to reply that this was not possible it was somehow difficult to explain why the fundamental precept of once a member of a kibbutz always a member of the kibbutz, entitled to all its privileges as well as obligations, did not apply to him. And while recognising that the question was to some extent a 'try on' there were uneasy stirrings when a West African loudly asked where his gold watch was while gesticulating towards the wrist of the man sitting next him at breakfast.

'But I thought we were all equal,' he said into a shocked silence.

These things, however, were merely irritations, indicating a gulf but fairly simply put right. What was more serious was the racial problem that, against all their expectations and in spite of all their efforts, began to grow up in Israel. I do not think it had ever occurred to them that they might be equated with the West. They felt so strongly their own identity as Israelis that they were certain it must be plain to everyone else that this was their allegiance and nothing else. But to some extent a man is a prisoner of the colour of his skin, and though many Israelis were dark it seemed to the sensitive black man that those who mattered to him were not. This attitude was complicated for the Israeli himself by internal tensions which were beginning to show towards the Oriental immigrant. There were families who would have viewed with strong disapproval their daughter making a 'mixed' marriage, not between Jew and non-Jew but between European and Oriental. Deborah, that old warrior, told of her anger with a near relative because he had strongly objected to his daughter marrying a man whose origin was North African. If this was a matter of tension within the society itself, it would naturally be even more so when one of those involved came from outside Israel and was not a Jew. So some of those from West Africa, alive to any possibility of a slight, had little difficulty in finding occasion for it.

There were some who found affronts when there was absolutely no reason for it, and to the Israelis this was both saddening

ISRAELI GIRL

139

and angering. The Hebrew word meaning 'black' was used quite naturally by the Israelis in conversation when talking about the Africans. It was used in a purely descriptive sense and meant nothing but what it said. Yet suddenly, out of the blue, this word began to take on sinister connotations for the African students. No one knew quite how this had happened or why, but once begun there was no going back on it. African students, knowing very little Hebrew, who heard this word—and they became very sensitive to it—immediately felt certain they were being insulted. No amount of explanation could persuade them otherwise. So the Israelis began to warn their children that this word, which was in common everyday use, was a bad word and must not be said in front of the students. This then became a vicious circle, for when they tried to persuade the Africans that they were innocent of offence the reply was: 'Why then do you tell your children not to use it?' One of the instructors even had a dog which was known by the Hebrew equivalent of 'Blackie', and so difficult had things become that he felt compelled to change its name.

One day Gershon found himself concerned with an incident of this kind. A particularly difficult student, who was apt to look for offence where none was to be found, saw a notice asking for blood donors. He felt certain that if he went and offered his blood it would be refused because he was black, and he determined to make an issue of this. So, before he went to the hospital, he found a photographer whom he persuaded to come with him and whose function was to take a picture at the precise moment when the doctor refused to accept the gift of African blood. It would be good propaganda.

Together student and photographer marched down the street to the hospital. The student pushed open the door and strode in. He rolled up his sleeve and advanced on the nurse in charge, striking an attitude which would make it plain in the photograph what was happening.

The nurse glanced at him. 'Please sit down,' she said. 'We'll take you next.'

Flabbergasted the student sank into a chair. It was not true then, they had not even looked surprised to see him and they were taking his blood in the most ordinary, calm fashion.

When he returned to the college where he happened to be living he told the story everywhere. They had taken his blood. He told it to Gershon. Gershon looked at him, this man who had demanded to be treated as an equal yet had behaved like a child.

'You don't think they used it?' he said. 'They poured it down the drain as soon as you left.'

Gershon gave no quarter. He rightly felt that these men and women had sooner or later to face the reality of the world in which they lived. They could not demand both independence and protection, nor expect to be cushioned against insults when insults were, regrettably, in common currency among humanity. So when they came to him with complaints of slights and offences, both real and imagined, he would reply:

'Certainly. I don't doubt it happened. And it will happen again, and again. Because that's the way the world is. What are you going to do about it?'

What they did about it varied with each man. At lunch one day in the training college, where students from many different countries were gathered in the middle of their courses before being dispersed again all over the country, we heard Israeli girls who waited at table being summoned in a rude and hectoring manner by African girl students.

'It is a great shock to the African girls,' we were told, 'when they first arrive and find themselves being waited on by "white" girls. This reversal of what has always seemed to them the established order casts them into confusion. When they begin to recover we find that their reaction is to bully the white girls unmercifully.'

It seemed unfair that the Israelis, who were traditionally innocent of any offence in this matter *vis-a-vis* the African countries, should nevertheless be suffering from the results of the years of colonial domination! But they were capable of accepting and understanding it; what seemed sadder still was that old bitternesses and ancient wrongs should be so closely nursed that the only thought was to wreak revenge on new friends as well as old foes.

We, too, had our moments both of pleasure and of pain. It was satisfying to be greeted by a high-powered Jamaican delegation as though we were long-lost brothers because we were British and Christian. Singularly nice men, of considerable distinction in their own country, they had come to Israel seeking for inspiration and advice in dealing with their own youth problems. We found this wounding, that they should have to turn away from Britain, which they admired, because they felt that Britain no longer had anything to offer them which was of constructive value when it came to dealing with the problems of the young. But when they told us how they felt we could not but agree. Where in Britain were they to find the new ideas which would help them to involve thousands of young unemployed Jamaican lads in the service of their own country? Who in Britain was able to tell them how to canalise and use for the common good the idealism of the young, or the ways in which this idealism could be nurtured? In Israel at least these were acceptable ideas.

But there were other places, more devious, where our national paths crossed. One moring we found an African sitting in the lounge of our hotel. We greeted him cordially and were somewhat put out by the dour, scowling look which he directed at us. He said nothing and we passed him by. When Hilal arrived to collect us for the day and we had followed him out over the window sill to the car we returned to the subject of the African.

'Do you know, Hilal, who that man was sitting in the hotel lounge?'

He looked surprised. 'Don't you know who that is? That's General China. Mau Mau. From Kenya.'

It was our turn to look surprised. We understood a little now of the absence of greeting.

'What's he doing here?' we asked, and Hilal began to tell us.

It seemed that General China, in company with some others from Kenya (this was before Kenyan independence), had been smuggled secretly out of the country to undertake an unspecified training in Israel. What it was we could only guess for Hilal would not tell us. However, he had apparently been responsible for teaching them topography.

When they arrived they were conveyed in conditions of great secrecy to a camp in the interior of Israel which was unidentified. No one at all was supposed to know who they were, what they were there for, or even that they were there at all. All went well for some months, then one morning in late May the mail arrived as usual. Through each letter box in each billet, correctly addressed to each Kenyan, there dropped a letter bearing on its reverse side the arms of Her Majesty's Embassy. Inside was a formal invitation to attend the Queen's Birthday cocktail party at the British Embassy.

Hilal could not understand why we laughed until the tears began to roll down our faces. He had told us the story more as an

illustration of the continuing perfidy of the British and because he was
genuinely puzzled as to why they resented Israel doing this form of
training than because he thought it amusing. After all the British
had not been fooled. They had known all the time who was in Israel,
and why, and where, and they had just let them carry on with the
charade. And, final insult, they had reminded the Kenyans, tacitly
but deliberately, that they were still members of the Commonwealth
owing allegiance to its Head. Presumably it was for this reason that
General China had come out of hiding and was now sitting openly in
our hotel. Presumably too it contributed to his refusal to greet us
with a cheerful good morning!

One morning we left Tel Aviv for a day visiting various communal settlements to the south. At about noon we drove into a
kibbutz which made a point of accepting foreign trainees, and where
there were known to be some West Africans from French-speaking
territories. The living quarters of the kibbutz were set among fine
trees, and as we drove up the kibbutzniks were coming in from their
morning's work to a mid-day meal. This was a religious kibbutz so
all the men wore the small round skull cap, or kippur, which was
the outward sign of orthodoxy. Among them, conspicuous by their
vividness and their physical grace, were some young Africans.
Above their shining black faces the normal, unaesthetic stitched
cloth hat in a shade of bright blue looked suddenly exotic and dash-
ing. When we greeted them their splendid white teeth flashed in the
friendliest of smiles. They came from Niger and Dahomey and they
were all very young.

Later, after a substantial meal eaten communally in the big dining-
hall, we visited two of these young men at work. They were concerned at this moment with the poultry section of the kibbutz,
where hundreds of chickens were incubated, grew up, fumed and
muttered in batteries and produced eggs which were then graded.
In contrast to some that we had met these young West Africans
were simple and unsophisticated and ready to return to their
own countries to farm. Watching them as they prepared the chicken
food and then picked their way carefully over the milling bodies of
the rushing, squeaking baby chicks to distribute it in the containers
one could see no distaste for the job but only satisfaction. Trial and
error had worked out a training that was down to earth and avoided
most of the pitfalls which had at first beset it. The overseas students
were given a chance to build their own equipment in wood, which

would be the raw material of their own country, instead of taking home the impression that all modern chicken houses must of necessity be concrete or iron, which is the case in Israel. They were encouraged to discuss their problems at home and to try to work out reasonable solutions in the light of what they saw in the kibbutz. Above all it was recognised that the highly complex, very efficiently organised farming of the kibbutz was not necessarily transplantable, but that the attitude of mind towards work which characterised all kibbutzim was.

'Do you feel that you have learned a lot?' we enquired of the young man from Niger in our bad French.

'Mais oui. J'ai appris quelquechose,' he answered cautiously and gave us his lovely, flashing, warm smile.

If the overseas students had begun to bring problems with them more disturbing, more insidious and more far-reaching tensions were those which were starting to appear within Israel itself. It was certain that the presence of the Oriental Jews had not been anticipated, at least not in the large numbers which since the 1950s had begun to weigh the balance against those from the occident. Originally problems of race and class had been unknown, and the only passport which a man needed to carry as his right to entry was the fact that he was a Jew. The early population entry had been in any case highly selective. But, uneasily, it was beginning to be seen that the coming of the Oriental Jews had made a difference, however unwillingly this was conceded, however much it might still be denied. For the groups that were now arriving at Haifa on the immigrant ships were not dedicated groups already self-selected by that very dedication, they might be a whole cross-section of a population from North Africa, bad as well as good, or even with the good already creamed off to seek refuge in France. Many of the immigrants now coming had relatives or friends already in Israel, and through them the grape-vine transmitted news of conditions within the state. It was no longer possible, as it had once been, to transfer whole sections directly from the ship to a new moshav or the semi-barren borders of the Negev. Although inducements were held out to persuade immigrants to go on the land, there were increasingly those who had no intention of doing so and were ready to make straight for family connections in Tel Aviv or Jerusalem as soon as the boat docked. It was not now so unusual for an immigrant to say: 'Certainly not. I won't farm in the Negev. I have relatives in the city.' While we were in Haifa there was, in fact, in the port a newly arrived immigrant ship on which there was a strike—the passengers refusing to come ashore if they were to be sent to build up new rural communities. Israel cannot dictate to her immigrants, she can only hope to persuade, persuasion backed by substantial government assistance to those who do choose to work on the land.

More difficult still were the stirrings of class tensions within the country for the first time. There was truth in the whisper that those of a darker skin, or from some countries of origin, were not encouraged to pay court to girls from good European families. The kibbutz had pioneered mixed marriages, but the very phrase indicated a self-consciousness about the subject which was not the climate of the classless society. One of our guides, with unusual frankness, told of the heart-searching that he and his wife went through because his son at school had Oriental friends who came from illiterate families.

'I do not want to make a difference,' he cried in real anguish. 'But I want the best for my son, and it will keep him back in his education if his friends have no background of knowledge or culture.'

On another occasion we took tea with an official of some standing in a Ministry and his wife and we listened with the sadness of recognition to their tale of the iniquities of the Yemeni neighbours, once servants, who had bettered themselves and moved into the flat next door. It was all there, the indignation that those who were considered inferior should somehow have managed to acquire material equality, the habits which were inimical, noise, smell and lack of consideration.

SMALL BOY LEARNING

We were told by responsible people that it was in the police that the beginnings of an under-privileged class were to be seen. Increasingly the sabra, the young man born in the country, was leaving the police and his place was being taken by young Oriental immigrants to whom the job was a status symbol conferring the compensation of power. The more this happened the more it changed the nature of the police, and the more the nature changed the less likely it was that the good young sabra would join the force. So the vicious circle could go on.

As in other countries these distinctions did not show themselves to any extent among the student population, or in the formal and idealistic communities within the society. In the kibbutz, with its philosophical dedication to equality, there was no difference between man and man when it came to colour. But the kibbutz population is a comparatively small percentage of the whole, and it seems as yet to have failed to spread the influence of its ideas widely among the ordinary people. Here, as in other countries, the sensitive areas were sex and work, and some jobs were undoubtedly coming to be considered as being more appropriate to the Oriental immigrants than others. The countering factor to this attitude was the comradeship and democracy of the Army, where men, and for the most part women, may have differed in their attainments but were, most urgently, equal in their value to the total community. It sometimes seemed that in a curious perverted way Israel's enemies were also her friends, and that had she not had this strong, cohesive cement of a perpetual threat on her borders the divisions within might have been very much more apparent. But threats are not intended to serve constructive purposes, and Israel would have much preferred to face a hard struggle with internal problems rather than the minute to minute possibility of real destruction.

None of these problems are as yet major ones, but they are there and Israelis are aware of them. Gershon used to say that he felt Israel's role in the world was to make miracles: a 'nes' is a miracle in Hebrew. It may be that it is even good that Israel should find herself afflicted with some of the problems which afflict us all, so that she may make a miracle and help us towards solutions.

There was one section of Israel's population, however, whose problems were of quite a different nature from all the others. These were the Arabs, of whom the greater number lived in the northern

areas of Galilee. As long as the outside Arab world remained re-
solutely hostile Israel's Arab citizens would continue to be a source
of trauma to Israelis. They could not expel them, to add to their
enemies and destroy the Jewish case for friendship: they could not
fully accept them, perhaps to find that they had prepared their own
Trojan Horse. When we said something to Gershon about Arab
refugees his reply was succinct and bitter: 'Arab refugees! All
Israelis are refugees.' Yet the relationship that existed between
those whose concern it was to work with the Arab farmers and
the men who were their colleagues and pupils was, on the surface
at least, warm and friendly, and we were occasionally reminded
that the Arabs had never, in fact, persecuted the Jews as did the
Christians. We travelled through some of the great sweeping, rolling
hill country beyond Haifa with the man who was agricultural advisor
to Arab farmers in that area and the burden of his conversation was:
'If only we could be friends with the Arabs what might we not do
together?' But even with his own charges, quite apart from those
over the borders, difficult questions of the rights and risks of citizenship hovered always unspoken at the back of men's minds. It
was one of his young men who gave vent to the plaintive cry that
he was lonely because all his friends had gone into the Army em-
phasising finally for him that with manhood had come also a realisation of his separateness.

Where for the young Israeli the land occupied a special place in
his collective thinking, this could no longer be so for the young
Arab. These boys were not encouraged to go on the land, for the
farms were too small and the opportunities too limited. But it was
also true that Arab fathers, for whom the land was not the exciting
new opportunity that it was for many Jewish fathers, felt that it
would indeed be a waste to give his son an education and then make
him farm. Education was for other ends, for the entry into the more
sophisticated world of commerce or trade or a profession. So that
when an Arab schoolboy, speaking good English and ready to
assail us with curious questions, answered bitterly our query as to
whether he would eventually become a farmer with the words:
'Farms? Where are our farms?' we were not wholly convinced that
even had they been there he would necessarily have embraced the
life of toil and simplicity that this work demanded.

This school was situated very near the border, and served one of
the small hill towns which lay practically over the frontier itself. We

147

were invited to have lunch with some of the town dignitaries, and the moment we drove up the steep, narrow streets, at the same time squalid and picturesque, where the women in bright dresses and white head scarves were collecting for a funeral, we felt ourselves to be in a different atmosphere, back again in the indefinable strangeness of the Middle East.

The meal they gave us had the full splendour of an Arab meal. Great heaped dishes of rice and meat and vegetables appeared after long intervals. We sat on a square verandah, open on one side to a courtyard where climbing plants and scrambling children meandered in the sun. The woodwork was painted blue. I had been told earlier, when gazing at an Arab village in Jordan with similiar blue woodwork that this colour was a protection against the devil. The women, of course, did not appear. Constraint lay thick on all of us. Our Arab hosts spoke English as though they were returning at last to a tongue that they had long been debarred from using. They wanted to speak it, and to be congratulated on their facility with the language. It was curious to be with people who were avid for what we could tell them, but though we would dearly have loved to return this courtesy a sense of obligation to our Jewish guide made us hesitate to ask any of the questions to which we should have liked to have known the answers: how did they live here, with their brothers in blood only a stone's throw away yet utterly divided from them? We hinted at something of this, asking how it was possible to keep the children from straying across the frontier. They smiled at us, and much of the unspoken thoughts that were in both our minds went into that smile, and said that the small boys did sometimes slip across; they were brought back, or sent back and punished... it was all very casual and nothing at all was really said. But sitting there, in square armchairs ranged round the walls of the square room, with the quiet sunshine outside filled at intervals with the sudden squawking of a scrawny chicken, there was no sight or sound to remind us that we were in the frontier zone of two countries who were not yet at peace. The Israeli Army, if it was here, was not in evidence, life was normal and humdrum and the tensions that there were in that little room were the tensions of men who recognise that they must learn to live together rather than the wariness of those who have set their hearts against doing so.

Later, in another district, we took coffee one morning with a Christian Arab farmer in the small house which lay in the middle

CYPRESSES

of his farm. This was quite a different occasion, though it too treated us to Arab courtesy and hospitality. But this time we felt that our Jewish guide was in no way excluded. Indeed it was obvious from the warmth of the greeting given him that he was a valued and well-liked friend.

Here no English was spoken, and while we drank thick sweet coffee and ate sticky, cloying sweets the conversation was translated from English to Hebrew to Arabic and back again the same way. The old man chuckled over his pipe, while his son, who had come back with an agricultural degree to help his father, discussed

149

the problems of the land and the weather and the machinery which was his special interest, and the women pressed on us more and yet more sweetmeats. When we left they handed to our guide some magnificent lettuces as a gift and he turned to us with pride: ' I don't know why it is,' he said, 'but the Arabs grow much better lettuces that the Jews!'

On the whole though, looking round, this did not seem to apply to much else, though later we saw some fine Arab vineyards. The age-old pace of fathers and fathers' fathers on this land could not so easily be speeded up. It was possible for those who came from without, to whom all farming was unexplored country, to accept new methods without question. They barely realised that they were new methods in the agricultural sense, it was all strange to them and one way of beginning was as good as another. But the men who had grown up to accept the land as their birthright and traditional ways of cultivating it as the established laws did not find it easy to desert the husbandry of their ancestors. For them too the perspective differed; they were not creating a new land but conserving all that was left to them of an old one.

The Dan cinema in Tel Aviv lay just across the road from our hotel, and at meals or when relaxing in our room we could, if we wished, have it constantly under observation. Increasingly as time went on we found ourselves fascinated by this rendezvous and the interesting sociological phenomenon that it presented to our gaze. We would come back from a strenuous day in a kibbutz or among the moshavim, filled with a sense of the thrusting, dedicated, purposeful life of young Israel, to find the steps of the Dan cinema overflowing with a milling, aimless throng of untidy-haired, leather-jacketed youths. All day this crowd ebbed and flowed, occasionally buying tickets and squeezing through the lobby to view some horrific epic, but more often simply using the cinema as a convenient place to lounge around, meet their friends and regard with bold, cynical eyes the passing traffic of the streets. These too were young Israelis, but one had seen their counterparts in many other cities of western Europe and wondered what kind of portent this gathering could be.

With the growth of her cities and the changing nature of her immigrants it was becoming increasingly obvious that Israel was not wholly immune from the malaise of youth which affected other countries. The pioneering purpose which had built the nation and which still imbued a large percentage of its young people found no echo in the breasts of the boys outside the Dan cinema, and even among the young whose idealism still glowed brightly it was not necessarily in the ways of their fathers that they wanted to give it expression.

'I carried messages for the Haganah at the age of fourteen,' said one mother. 'Now my daughter's only problem is studying – and even that she doesn't do very well.' She said it with a sense of loss, something had gone out of life she felt. Her daughter had, faintly, disappointed.

For the present the Army was capable of solving even the problems of the Dan cinema. At eighteen, for the dangerous years from eighteen to twenty-one, the Army would take these young men and press them into acceptable citizens. Unless that is they were already young delinquents with a prison sentence behind them. But this was a way of muffling the problem rather than a solution to it, for a constant standing Army absorbing every young member of the population is the result of a very uneasy political background; the hopes of any country thus placed must surely be that the time will come when it is possible to abolish this preparation for war. The paradox is that the military arm solves the social problems while the society must work for conditions in which the military arm is no longer necessary. Will it then become obvious that we have given little constructive thought to the social realities of a peaceful society? It is ironic that the state we all long for can often be the one for which we are least prepared.

It was with considerable reluctance that Israel was being forced to consider the possibility that agriculture might have to share its pride of place with industry. But the reluctance was not on the part of the young. The old values which were group values, devoting all to the community and personally recreating the land, were being forced by circumstances to change. New cities, like Arad in the northern Negev and Ashdod on the

SOCIAL WORKER

coast, needed pioneers too, of a different and more individual kind: young doctors, nurses, dentists, craftsmen, who would be prepared to take their skills out of the older, more comfortable, life into the hard, often isolated, existence of a brand-new desert city. Reflections of the conflict which this shift of emphasis involved echoed and re-echoed across Israel while we were there. It was a shock to some to recognise that Israel, after all, had no sacred right to be free from the problems that beset other societies, and that having set herself to be a twentieth-century nation she had thereby tied herself to the wheel of twentieth-century development. There seems no reason why an industrialised society should not be as just a society as an agricultural one, for it is not where men live but how that determines this, but it does appear to be true that cities are often felt to be immoral in themselves. How much does this feeling help to create the thing it fears? How far, I wonder, does our age-old acceptance of cities as wicked, from the time of Sodom and Gomorrah down through the Pilgrim's Progress and beyond, inhibit our efforts to deal with their problems and predetermine our attitude to many of their iniquities? But the more highly urbanised and industrialised we become the more necessary it is that the younger generation should not be made to feel that pioneering is only valid if it is tough and physical and actively connected with the land. There is much social pioneering still to be explored. When we spoke a little of this with an elderly Israeli, whose youth had been one of hard and exciting physical endeavour, his reply was: 'Pioneering is not getting there first; it is remaining and enduring.' Maybe, and he had done his full share of both; but for the young it is not surprising that getting there first still seems to take priority. It must be made possible that it is not only remaining and enduring in situations which their fathers pioneered that is left to them, but that there are also opportunities where they too can get there first.

One afternoon we were taken out by a very intelligent and charming young Army officer, a woman, to see a Nahal in action. This was an élite conscript Army group who had chosen in the second year of their military training to form an agricultural Nahal and work on the land. In this instance they were not pioneering a new settlement but were attached to a kibbutz which was itself very short of man-power. This was a recognised pattern and it was a very valuable one to the kibbutzim, whose manpower situation did not keep pace with their agricultural development.

It was, in fact, an unfortunate day to go, for the rain had just started to fall and the kibbutz, when eventually we reached it after several diversions because of flooding, was so much under water that all work in the fields had stopped. The young soldiers were in their huts and a general air of sodden dispiritedness lay over everything. We were put into the recreation room to wait while the sergeant, who was in bed, was aroused and could talk to us. When he came we asked if we could speak to one or two of the members of the Nahal, and at last two girls and a young man turned up. They were quiet, uncommunicative and very ordinary. There was a feeling in the air that the kibbutz, while needing their labour, did not welcome them into its fellowship, and that they lived on the edge of the community, with it but not of it.

I had been interested in the position of the women in all the communal settlements, and I questioned the girls about this as well as I could. They shrugged their shoulders; yes, they said, in theory they had equality and could do the same jobs as men, but in practice they were well aware that it was simply not so. In practice they ended up with the duller jobs, the routine jobs, the traditional jobs.

It was for me a big disappointment in Israel that this society, of which one had heard so much and seen such splendid pictures, did not seem in fact to have resolved any of the dilemmas which the twentieth century has created in the role of women. There is an unease noticeable among the girls in the Nahal, and the failure rate is much higher than for boys. There are crises in the kibbutzim, many resulting from psychological unrest among the women. Even in an industrial kibbutz it is difficult to find what is known as 'productive' work for the women, and she often finds herself released from personal domestic chores not to work in imaginative new fields but to engage in public chores. The Army accepted all young male illiterates and educated them, but it did not accept all young female illiterates, because it was felt to be too expensive to do so and, in any case, they often came from orthodox families which raised complications.

Of course there were many opportunities for women in Israel and the possibility of reaching the highest ranks in any profession, but this is not unusual nowadays and it did not alter my feeling that this was a patriarchal society. The attempt to emancipate the women was based, as it so often seemed to me to be, on a false premise which could be clearly seen in the phrase 'unproductive' work as

YOUNG GIRL

applied to many of the main functions of a woman's life. The effort
required is not so much to free the woman to work alongside the
men in male jobs as to educate the men in the real value of the work
that is traditionally and primarily the woman's. As long as the things
that she knows in her heart to be important are considered second-
class jobs, so long will the woman feel psychologically uneasy in a
world that is orientated to this philosophy. What, after all, could be
more productive than producing and training the generations that
are to take over. It would not seem to me a retrograde step to recognise that the sexes are complementary rather than competitive,
geared to different ways of dealing with life to complete a harmon-
ious whole, and that women are capable of a wide range of activities
and need have guilt complexes about none of them. Perhaps more
marriages took a real step towards partnership when young fathers
began to change the nappies and wash the dishes than ever did when
young mothers began to go out to work.

I thought of Dan's mother, about whom we knew nothing except that for her the whole splendid pioneering venture of abandoning all that was stable to go out in search of a lifelong vision had been a hard slow struggle. How much of it was martyrdom, the frustration of feeling her contribution to the new life unnoticed or under-valued? For so often it was the women's values that were being overthrown, and the women themselves conditioned, with or without their co-operation, to a man's world. But both sets of values are needed, and both are valid. It is considered, by women as well as by men, that the conversation of women together, about children, about household affairs, about the day to day matters of the neighbour-hood, is trivial, infinitely less worthwhile than male talk about business or sport. It does not seem a just assessment. The minutiae of life are as essential to its goodness as the broad sweep; the values shown in relation to children and neighbours may be more serious and worthwhile than those displayed in big business. The effort is to drag one side into the world of the other, and this is true of both sides; but surely some kind of co-operative interchange is much more effective in releasing a wider range of creative talents in both parties, and to make this possible both worlds may have to accept some reorientation and not just one.

It is not the fact that the women still seem to be confined to many of the domestic chores that is the disillusionment in Israel, it is that the domestic chores themselves are still regarded as boring, frustrat-ing, perhaps even degrading, if necessary, jobs. In a penal camp in California, which we visited a few years ago, in which young deli-quents were organised to fight forest fires, they had reversed this set of values. Kitchen Patrol was considered the most responsible job within the camp. A boy had to work up to it as an honour, for what could be more important work than that on which the whole health and hygiene of the camp depended. So it was towards the end of their time, when they had shown themselves to be ready for it, that they were promoted to this work. The atmosphere of this camp was one of purpose and effort and morale was very high. No one, at any stage, had a job which he felt to be second rate. The trouble here was that this way of looking at things was totally at variance with the outside world, and may well have made their return to it in due time a minor, or perhaps a major tragedy. Our society creates its own problems, they do not just fall on us from the hand of an uncaring Providence.

155

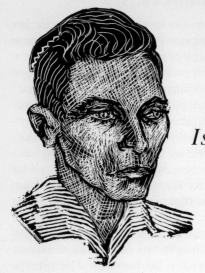

CHAPTER VIII

Israeli independence:
Jewish jeopardy

SHIMON

SHIMON had refused to take tea with us because he had had a late lunch and the three hours that must separate the eating of meat products with those of milk were not yet up. He sat looking at us very quietly out of gentle light blue eyes and said that he considered that residence in Israel was basic in the religion of any good Jew.

'How do you mean?' we asked a little puzzled.

He answered calmly: 'If you don't come to Israel, you are not a Jew.'

'But,' we spluttered, taken aback by the absolute certainty with which he spoke, 'there must be lots of good Jews in countries like America and Britain for whom it just isn't a practical proposition to come to Israel.'

'They have decided not to come,' he said. 'They have broken faith with The Land. It is their own choice but they no longer belong.'

We looked at each other rather aghast, then my husband, hoping to restore what we would have considered a sense of proportion to the conversation, said: 'You don't mean to say that you think one of these young layabouts outside the Dan cinema is a better Jew than a rabbi in America just because he happens to have been born in Israel.'

'Yes,' said Shimon. 'I do say it.'

So here before us, in extreme terms, lay the dilemma of Judaism.

156

Shimon was an orthodox, religious Jew of Belgian origin. We had asked him if he would be willing to come and tell us something about the religious Jews, because increasingly, as we went about Israel, we met the distinction between 'religious' and 'non-religious' and some confusion had grown up in our own minds. It was a curious paradox that in the land which had been the cradle of so much of the world's spiritual heritage there seemed fewer outward signs of a relationship between man and God than in any other country that we had visited. In the old villages and towns the spire of a church or minaret of a mosque might point skywards, but in all the neat new villages that scattered the hills of Galilee and Jerusalem and spread over the coastal plains there was no visible sign of any concern with spiritual things. They might have been villages without souls. Undoubtedly some of this arose from the past history of the Jews. They had been a people who lived always as a minority among foreigners, aware of their own insecurity and of the thin crust which separated them from persecution. The soul and essence of their difference lay in their religious life and they had come to feel that the less conspicuous their synagogues were the better. Not

GALILEE VILLAGE

for them the splendid flaunting of their beliefs in huge piles of ela-
borately carved stone, the gilded magnificence of sacred vessels
carried in open procession through the streets; their places of worship must look externally as like an ordinary dwelling place as possible, and indeed they often were a part of just such a home. Long-
established traditions die hard, and many of the rows of square,
white new buildings may have concealed a synagogue in their midst,
but one was also left with the feeling that many did not.

Again, in contrast to its history, the climate of Israel was more
openly agnostic than we had expected. A large percentage of the
men who spent time and energy to show us their work made plain
at some time or another in conversation that they were anti-religious.
It seemed difficult to find any middle course between those who
fanatically believed and those who were almost as dedicated in
their disbelief. Yet for all, as indeed for us, the issue was not such a
simple one as this because the stuff of their belief was also the stuff
of their own history. So that the great festivals, which were religious
festivals, celebrated also battles and deliverances in the history of
their people, and it was a history which had become curiously near
to them in time because of a telescoping forgetfulness which cut out
of many memories all the experiences in the Diaspora. The return
to The Land, which all whatever their beliefs held to be a fundamental right, even the faith which had kept them separate throughout two thousand years, depended on their belief that they were
a Chosen People to whom the land belonged. But chosen by a God
and promised The Land by a God in whom many of them did not
believe.

The religious element may have been a small one, but it was one
of considerable political importance in a complex balance of power,
sufficient importance to ensure that Israel was a religious and not a
secular state. The rigid dietary laws, laid down in the time of Moses,
were observed everywhere. One might not eat meat products and
milk products at the same meal, or within three hours of each other;
none of the flesh of the pig or of any other unclean beast was permitted. The Sabbath was strictly observed, resulting in a complete
stoppage of all public transport from sundown on Friday to sundown
on Saturday, except in Haifa where a sensible compromise had been
arrived at with the considerable Arab population of the city that the
Jewish bus drivers work on the Friday — which is the Moslem holiday — and that the Arab drivers do the work on Saturday. All

MOSQUE IN OLD JAFFA

marriage was religious, which meant in effect that no marriage to a
non-Jew was valid, and all babies born out of wedlock, whether
Jewish or not, were forbidden to marry Jews. It was the religious
party which had enforced the use of the Hebrew alphabet at a time
when there was some consideration whether the Roman alphabet
might not have advantages for the new nation, and in many other
ways, both large and small, the humanist and materialist state lived
in a religious framework. It could be that this was good for no one,
driving men away from spiritual consideration by constant political
irritations.

While we were there a storm arose over the matter of the new
Israeli steamship, *Shalom*, which illustrated some of the dilemmas

and tensions. Israel was anxious, naturally, to develop her links with the rest of the world, and also to add to her earning power. A national shipping line was one obvious way of doing this, and the Zim line recently had built a new, fast and very modern liner. She was to ply between countries in Europe and America and, naturally, her passenger list would not be exclusively Jewish. The whole object of such a ship was to attract traffic from among people who might otherwise be unacquainted with the achievements of Israel. This raised, however, a question about feeding. On a crack liner, competing on the open market for passengers with other countries, would their business chances not be reduced if the food was all kosher? The shipping line thought they would and applied for permission to have two kitchens, one kosher, one not, so that they could suit all tastes.

However, they knew that if this application went to the appropriate office in Jerusalem it would be refused, because all public food in Israel, and on Israeli airlines, etc., is kosher, and this is an area in which the religious party have control. So the shipping line went to the appropriate Rabbinical office in America for permission and got it. To non-Israelis it is a curious situation where appeal could be made to a court outside one's own country for a ruling which it is known would not be permitted inside it! The shipping line, accepting the permission to have two kitchens as valid, then went ahead to prepare the ship on this basis. Even so it meant a vast amount of work because the thickness of steel between the two kitchens to ensure that there would be no contamination was laid down to the last millimetre.

The story, of course, did not end there. The Rabbinical office in Jerusalem hearing what had been going on, was not only outraged at the suggestion that the ship should not be entirely kosher but deeply affronted that their authority should have been by-passed. There was a tremendous political row which shook the government and the American edict was rescinded. The *Shalom* became kosher. As far as I know she is still.

The words 'religious' and 'non-religious' used constantly in connections that seemed often to us to be more legalistic than spiritual made us uneasy. One evening, driving back to Tel Aviv with Hilde, the young Army officer who had been showing us the Nahal, she began to

SMALL RELIGIOUS BOY

talk about religious boys in the units, and the difficulties involved with religious girls from very strict families. She was sympathetic and her English was perfect so I felt emboldened to ask her something which troubled me.

'When you talk about the "religious" boys does this mean that they show a difference in behaviour? Is it something that makes them try for some kind of a different moral standard from the others?' It was difficult to put into words just what I meant without sounding rude or priggishly superior.

At first she looked rather puzzled. 'I don't understand what you mean,' she said.

I tried again. 'Well, I sometimes think that it seems more a case of obeying certain rules which aren't really anything to do with moral or spiritual behaviour...' I wished I had never started on such a delicate subject.

She was not affronted, however. She saw suddenly what I was trying to say.

'Oh no,' she said. "They don't behave any differently, but there are certain laws laid down that they must follow.'

She then went on to probe us as to what we would understand by the use of the word 'religious' in connection with a person we knew. It was at this point that the controversy which has started to grow up in Britain around this same word began to come into focus. When I thought carefully to answer her it seemed that it might be true for us also that what we understood by the word 'religious' might not be at all the same as what we understood by the word Christian. What I was looking for was a loving standard of behaviour rather than obedience to certain ritual rules.

But Shimon, an orthodox Jew himself, when we touched with some diffidence on this distinction, did not hesitate.

' I don't like "religious" and "non-religious",' he said. 'It is whether one is Jewish or not Jewish.'

'When non-religious socialists attack us for taking this position,' he continued, 'I ask them: "Why did you come to Israel? Why didn't you go to Uganda or Argentina, or stay and spread socialism in Europe? Because you are *Jews*".'

There are the outlines of a battle here, but it is not yet joined. The pointers are there, the frontiers are hardening, but outside pressure and the still-fresh miracle of the birth of the State act as strong cohesive factors. Israel herself has not yet decided, any more than the rest of the world, the answer to the age-old question. What is a Jew? but the new factor of an established Israeli nation- ality may hasten the moment when a decision will have to be made. When it is, what will be the effect on those outside, who have taken the conscious decision to remain outside? It is one of the fascin- ating problems of Israel, the dimensions of which are as yet only glimpsed here and there. in a discussion, a chance remark dropped in a cafe, an attitude of mind revealed in conversation. Even in London a very old and very distinguished Jew had said to us: 'I liked it better when it was Palestine,' and in Israel one of our guides told how he had come to Britain 'to help young Jews find their soul. He conceived them to be in a limbo, floating between the romantic vision of Israel and the reality of assimilation; ready to accept neither and inhabiting a position which became more amorphous and more soul destroying as time went on. Naturally he felt that they needed to be given the courage to opt for Israel, and he admit- ted that Israel needed them. He did not blame the young but their parents who put security and comfort and their privileged position in British society before the call of loyalty and faith which they owed to The Land. They looked on Israel as the keeper of their conscience. but they would not encourage their children to go there for fear they should find themselves and never return. But he went further than this, for he did not hesitate to say that they should face the realities of their own situation and, if indeed they felt that Britain was the homeland to which they belonged, then they should whole- heartedly permit their young people to be assimilated into the com- munity of the country of their birth.

As yet, however, Israel would in fact be hard put to it to survive if such clear-cut decisions were demanded of all her potential overseas citizens. Everywhere there is evidence of the enormous contrib- ution which outside wealth has made to the development and stab- ility of the new country. Much of the capital which has made the physical growth of the new villages possible has come from world Jewry through the Jewish Agency. For that matter the people themselves have often been enabled to come in this way too. Everywhere one goes one sees notices, on forests, on buildings, in institutions, among plantations, bearing witness to the gener- osity of groups from other countries, noticeably America, who have financed these projects. Mr C. preferred to ignore this evidence of non-Israeli, though of course not non-Jewish, interest in his country, whirling us rapidly past them, or even at times deliberately denigrating their contribution. He disliked the idea of being beholden to anyone not of Israeli citizenship, and this applied equally to those of his own faith. After a while one began to wonder how far Israel acted as the safety valve of overseas Jewry, in a sense enabling them to eat their cake and have it, and for how long Israel would wish to be in this position. Shimon and the orthodox may come to want to cast them off because they feel them to be evading their religious responsibilities; while the growing generations of sabras could come to feel that they are, quite simply, nothing to do with those outside and to equate them increasingly with the countries whose languages they speak and less and less as having any call upon Israel's attention. The choice may not lie with Israel, who as she stabilises herself in the modern world will become more independent of those outside who claim a special relationship, the choice may lie with world Jewry, who may have to make some painful decisions as to the claims on allegiance now that the vision is reality and they have, technically, repudiated it. Or is it possible to look further than this age of possessive nationalism and visualise the pioneering of a complicated system of dual nationalities on a new and much deeper level? It would be saddening if the Return, while signifying the beginning of a new era, ushered in also the end of the Jewish solidarity which has enabled a people to survive and inherit The Land; if increasingly those from outside feel, as the bewildered Dr Cohen did, 'I said to myself that I had come to a land of Gentiles.'

There was another curious side to the shifting, changing pattern of Israeli national life. Shimon was in fact a moderate in his religious position, and his passionate identity with Israel was shared by the great majority of his fellow citizens whatever their spiritual views. But by an ironic twist those most deeply committed to a purely religious life, to whom the Holy Land was a mystic article of faith, were the very ones who repudiated the State of Israel in all its political manifestations as being a desecration. The small groups in the Mea She'arim were of this persuasion, allowing the state no sovereignty, not even writing letters because the stamps belonged to the state, and so was the uncle of our Latvian friend who had felt that he could not accompany his family to a secular realisation of the Holy Land and had stayed behind to die in a concentration camp. Less extreme, but in their own way equally difficult to accommodate within a new nationalism, were the Jews of

Safad, a town situated in Galilee and one of the five holy cities. They fought for the state, but they would not break the law when it came to the Sabbath, fighting or no fighting. So they rested on the Sabbath and were killed by the enemy.

'If the non-religious want to attack the religious they always talk of the Mea She' arim and the extremists,' said Shimon. One could not help wondering whether, all unwittingly, the extremists had not foreshadowed one of the major problems of The Land. The extremists had found their own way out, but Israel had still to face the larger significance that was inherent in their action not just for them but for the whole Jewish community.

'Many Jews who were religious in the Diaspora, to avoid assimilation, cease to be religious when they come to Israel,' said Shimon. It was a nationality, a separate identity that they craved, and in the long years of the Dispersion the symbols of religion served to maintain their unique heritage in the face of a world that would otherwise have absorbed or exterminated them. But there is no need now for such self-defence. The problem of identity is solved for some, and could be solved for many more. Or it may be that a new and more complex problem of identity has been posed for those who find themselves caught between a religion that they do not sincerely share and a nationality that they do not care to don.

The Zionism of the early settlers was not, in fact, religious. They were humanist, communist, materialist, seeking a new social order in a country they felt to be rightfully theirs. The religion of the kibbutz is the kibbutz, and this may be a fundamental reason for their inability to attract a new manpower from outside. It is said that young Israelis look to Sweden as a model and a goal in the search for a classless, socialist society. Ironically the planes that carry them there to study the blue-print pass in mid-air the planes that bring young Swedes from their idyllic society to Israel in search of a soul. 'The Jewish contribution is to be an example to the rest of the world,' said Shimon. He may be right, but it is their spiritual heritage that has been the reason for their survival and the splendid enrichment of mankind; it is by no means certain that without a deepening and renewing of the spirit the material example will be able to emulate its tremendous past.

I went to Israel as a Christian, but it was not a matter of pilgrimage. I had not expected to be able to recreate a physical environment and indeed made no attempt to do so. Perhaps this was as well because it obviously did not occur to anyone that we might have a special interest in historical Christian sites, or, like Mr C., they hurried us past them quickly almost defying us to make an additional request for a stop. Had we attached importance to a physical Christian experience it would almost certainly have been disappointed. The visit to the church at Nazareth, where Mr C., at the special pleading of his wife, was persuaded to drop us for an hour, added nothing to our spiritual growth. The church, hideously mediocre architecturally, stood over a cave in the rocks which, we were assured, had been the home of the Holy Family when they returned from the flight into Egypt. The Arab Christian who showed it to us was glib and insincere, and the Americans who followed down the narrow stairs were clicking their cine cameras and whispering excitedly. There seemed no real evidence to equate this particular cave, or indeed any cave at all, with the early life of Christ, and the enormous new church which was in the process of building was interesting but totally unrelated in my heart to my particular spiritual experience. Nevertheless I did return from Israel with a new dimension to my Christianity, a deeper reality and understanding. Much of this was due to the conversation with Shimon. His quiet, dogmatic certainties, which were identical with those of his forefathers in the time of Christ, suddenly illuminated vividly the circumstances under which the gospel had first been preached and its revolutionary character.

The Jamaicans, who were sincere and practising Christians, had some difficulties about their weekends. They wished to have their Sunday free, and this was a proposition, entailing as it would two complete non-working days, which went against a fundamental of Gershon's philosophy of concentrated hard work. The Jamaicans were intrigued by the Jews and found them in many ways totally different from their expectations which were based on the

NUN AT NAZARETH

Old Testament. On the whole they found them very much nicer than they had expected! A major aspect of Judaism, in which it differed radically from Christianity, and one that interested the overseas students was its non-missionary character. They felt themselves free from any religious pressure, and many of them, with memories of the combination in their own countries of new knowledge and missionary endeavour going hand in hand, welcomed this at first. However, there came a moment when what was apparently a strength was revealed also as a weakness, especially to those, and there were many, for whom spiritual matters were still of importance. If it was the case that there was here a religious truth of great value why were the Jews not willing to share it? It was either not so vital as it was thought to be, or it was vital and they, the students, were deliberately being excluded from it. Accustomed to a world in which men who believed passionately in any idea felt impelled, whether for good or evil, to transmit this idea to others, they had a feeling that at the very end of acceptance there stood a barrier which was impassable.

We asked Shimon about this and his answer was revealing.

'We tried it once with the Samaritans,' he said, 'and it didn't work.' The Samaritans had been forced converts to Judaism under King David and later became persecutors of Judea. It was extraordinary to be eating bread and butter and drinking tea in a Tel Aviv hotel while Shimon cited as if it had happened yesterday something out of remote biblical history. We pressed him a little, however, as to whether it was ever possible for an individual to become a Jewish convert. He himself had told us of instances, not many but some, in kibbutzim when a non-Jewish young man or girl had wished to marry a young Jew, and of the complications that this created. Yes, he said, it was possible; it had happened, but they did not much like it and would certainly not encourage such a step. In fact every effort would be taken to make the actual act of conversion as difficult as possible. It would require a long period of study and training, and this would deliberately be made more difficult for a Gentile than the equivalent course of study might be for a Jew. But before that, when it seemed that the mind of the convert was irrevocably made up, there would be two questions asked which were fundamental. The first was: Can you observe very strict regulations? It would be expected, explained Shimon, that a convert keep to the last detail all the rules about diet, and regulations governing the Sabbath, the small day-to-day commandments for living that were laid down in the Mosaic Law. Where a born Jew might occasionally slip from perfection a convert would never be allowed this laxity. The second question was: Can you endure persecution? And this they would still ask, for a background of twenty centuries is not lightly laid aside. Provided the answers were satisfactory and the convert came through his rigorous training favourably, he would be accepted into the Jewish faith.

Shimon looked at us and his charming smile appeared for a moment on his grave young face: 'But he would still be regarded as a Goy by full-blooded Jews,' he said.

It was a fascinating, bemusing, and enlightening experience to be talking in terms of the first century and the twentieth century at one and the same time. Always the past and the future were inexorably intertwined. More than with most new countries this one felt as if it stood at a crossroads of history, maybe carrying our future forward as well as its own.

STAR OF DAVID

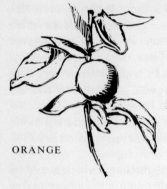

CHAPTER IX

From Dan to Beersheba

ORANGE

My HUSBAND got out of the car as Mrs C. came along the street towards us. He took off his hat and held open the door for her.

'No, no,' said Mr C. 'Just say "hello". We don't have all that sort of thing here.'

It was, however, no easier for us to forget the habits we had been accustomed to than it would have for Mr C. suddenly to take them up, so we still shook Mrs C. by the hand and said how glad we were to meet her, before making way for her to climb into the car.

Later it was Mrs C. who took us quietly aside and explained that we were embarrassing a man, whose name we did not in fact know, by calling him 'Mr Dov'. 'This is Dov,' had been our introduction and, uncertain whether it was his first or his last name, we had felt it better to play safe. Mrs C. was very tactful. 'We don't use Mr,' she said. 'Call him by his first name, which is Dov, or use Halev.' Halev means comrade. It seemed to be a choice between two embarrassments, ours or theirs, and the result was much wary treading on our part to avoid the use of any sort of name at all!

I have never actually found that the free use of a first name necessarily results in the friendliness and informality which it is intended to indicate. It is not what one calls a man that denotes ones feeling for him, it is rather the tone in which the name, any name, is said. And if, at first acquaintance every barrier is laid low there is no progression possible as friendship grows and deepens. Curiously enough Mr C., who first made plain to us that we were expected to conform in this matter, never suggested that we call him anything else but Mr C., and in fact I never knew what his other name was. Nevertheless, as we penetrated beyond his prickly exterior and

168

became accustomed to the absolutes in which he saw the world we grew to like and respect him. He would appear in the hotel lounge in the early morning, always punctual, always clad in an olive-green jacket knitted by his wife, to collect his quota of overseas students for the day and on our greeting him would give us a caustic, sardonic, but increasingly approving smile. Very little of the world outside Israel had reality any longer for Mr C. His dedication and his passion were for this land. When one met him one recognised in him, unconcealed, the rock of the Israeli spirit against which any outside storms would beat in vain. Mr C. might die on his land, but he would never desert it. What had once been a cause for him, as for so many others, had become a country into which they had put down as firm and as tenacious roots as any of the ancient olive groves that we passed on the way to the north.

Mr C. took us to Galilee, to Ayelet Hashahar. We did not go as far as Dan, which is further still, at the northermost tip of Israel, but in conversation something came up about frontiers and boundaries and we said without thinking, unconsciously aware of the ancient biblical limits, 'from Dan to Beersheba'. Mr C. was astonished. 'How did you know that?' he demanded, implying that we had no right to be acquainted with Israel's history. We were equally surprised to recognise that Mr C. did not seem to know that his country's historic past was also part of the tradition of Christian nations. We mumbled something about it being in the Bible, not quite certain whether we were entitled to claim a share in this Book or not. This happened quite frequently during our stay. Sometimes we found ourselves better acquainted with the doings of the patriarchs than our hosts and we felt curiously ashamed when this was so. Occasionally they told us tales which were already second nature to us without seeming to realise that we knew anything about them. Perhaps the Americans who come to Britain well versed in what they feel to be their own historical roots suffer also from this strange sensation of double vision when we at one and the same time show ourselves both forgetful of our heritage and affronted at their superior knowledge of it.

It was on the Galilee journey that we first made our acquaintance with fruit, in the Israeli sense, ubiquitous, all-pervading fruit. We had been told that Israel was a great fruit salad, and looking round we could understand what was meant by this. Everywhere, row upon row, the trees grew: oranges, grapefruit, clementines, guavas, and many more varieties and species. They were coming into season and the balls of yellow or gold or green hung heavily among the shining leaves. Very early on we collected our first gift of fruit, clementines to slake our thirst in the middle of the day. Each farmer whose trees we admired heaped generous handfuls of his produce on us, every house we stayed in gathered up the contents of their bowls and pressed them on us as a parting gift. It was wonderful fruit, sweet and juicy, coming to us straight from the trees which supplied the markets of the world; but we were only two, for no one else would share our fruit insisting that it was for us alone, and we could not manage more than half-a-dozen clementines a day. I had not realised what a problem this was going to pose until I tried to get rid of the surplus in what seemed to me a sensible and kindly way. One morning, in the hotel at Tel Aviv, as we were leaving for a day's outing, I filled a bag with oranges and presented it to the little chamber maid who did out our rooms. She spoke some English and had told me about her children and some of the difficulties of her life.

'Here, for the children,' I said to her and held out the bulging bag.

She looked appalled. I could not understand it. She refused with horror.

'Do you not like it?' she said. 'It is your fruit.'

I could see by her face that I had committed an error. Quite obviously she was less concerned with my thought for her children than with the possibility that I was insulting an Israeli product. I apologised and withdrew the bag, feeling impelled to take a clementine out and eat it there and then to show her that I had intended no disrespect.

The next day, when the bag was swollen by an extra gift and already those at the bottom were beginning to feel soft and pulpy, I decided to resort to more drastic measures. We were to be away, returning three days later, I would simply put the whole bag in the waste paper basket, thus making plain that I had done with it, and leave the hotel to deal with the fruit as it thought fit. I did this, and felt my spirits lighten as we drove off. For a short while at any rate I was unburdened by either gift or obligation. When we returned the room they had assigned to us was not the same, but when we opened the door one thing struck horribly familiar. There, on the bedside table, was my discarded, swollen, somewhat jaded bag of fruit.

TRIPOLI FARMER AMONG TOMATOES

Several times more I tried surreptitiously to drop it in a ditch, leave it casually behind a door, or in a car, but each time we had gone only a little way when the familiar cry rang out: 'You've left your fruit. How lucky that we saw it,' and kindly hands would give it back to me. In the end I was defeated. I accepted the perpetual burden and, like one condemned to carry the old man of the sea, I took it everywhere. I could not bring myself to take the one sure way to rid myself of it, to say: 'I've had enough, I do not want it,' and watch incredulous hurt come into those hospitable eyes.

Israelis live upon their own produce, and it is a matter of pride to do so as well as a matter of economic necessity. Tomatoes and cucumbers formed a staple salad, and great fields of cucumbers and tomatoes blanketed the plains. We stood among them at Purat, a village not far from the central border, while the agricultural extension worker discussed problems with the village chief. The people had come from Tripoli as a group about 1948 and he had managed, by strong leadership, to keep the group together ever since. Now we could see how they had prospered, looking out over the acres of tomato plants grown as tall as the women who worked up and down among their regular rows. The women still spoke to each other in their own language. This was a group which had managed to preserve a patriarchal structure for itself inside the democratic process of the state. But it was not without conflict and this came in the area of education. It was in the tradition of these people that the children, from an early age, helped on the land, and the cohesiveness of the group maintained respect for this tradition. The state, however, expected that the children would go to school, and in school they would learn knowledge which might divide them from their parents and disrupt the ancient customs. It was a ding-dong battle yet but inevitably the state would win.

It was one more piece in the kaleidoscope, the jigsaw of individuals creating groups and communities separating and merging, of strangers come home to a land which was not their own and natives become foreigners in their own towns, of aggressive pride and sensitive humility which made up the social pattern of Israel.

Though we did not get to Dan we did, in fact, travel to Beersheba. We were on our way further south still to Eilat, the new port which gives Israel access to the Red Sea. In the event, however, the day we left for the south the rains broke and the desert road through the Negev became impassible.

The rains had been awaited with some impatience because they were late. For us this had been a pleasure, giving us two weeks of clear, dry, sparkling weather at a season which might otherwise have been dull and wet, but for everyone else the coming of the rain was a matter of major importance and a good deal of

BUS STOP

concern. Water. Water. Water is Israel's main agricultural problem, and there is little enough in any case. It was therefore all the more surprising, when the rains did come, to find this part of the country flung into confusion. For Beersheba and its surrounding district are desert and reclaimed desert, and during the dry season its channels dry up and its wadis become filled with drifting sand. For seven years now the rainfall in Beersheba had been very small and, as everywhere in similar circumstances, human nature tends to forget and grow slack. Suddenly, in a fierce, wild storm the heavens opened and the rains fell. The water descended in a curtain which enclosed our bus and drove with hysterical slaps against the windows. Wadis filled up and great cataracts of brown water hurled down the shallow channels and rushed over the causeways which carried the road. A viscous dun mud appeared on either side of the tarmac, and rumours began to circulate among the bus passengers about blocked bridges and impenetrable floods. There

SHOP SIGNS

was no need of translation, such whispers have a common language and we were soon as well aware as anyone that ours might be the last bus to get through to Beersheba, or alternatively the first not to do so.

'We have had seven lean years, now perhaps we shall have seven fat ones,' said someone. 'Like the cows in Egypt,' we murmured, trying not to sound too smug!

When it loomed over the horizon, ghostly through the veils of rain, Beersheba had none of the romantic aura that I had always connected with that name. From a distance it resembled a shanty town and a defensive post rolled into one. Wireless masts and great numbers of Army vehicles competed with stark new buildings rising sheer out of desert sand. A low, untidy straggle, the town appeared to have no shape or form. As we drew into it, it assumed more the character of the American frontier west as one imagines it to have been in the early days. Half finished, or half begun, the new vying with the old; unmade roads and neon lights; camels and huge articulated trucks; Bedouins and Klondykers;

the sort of chaos which is the thrusting, harsh beginning of creation.

We climbed out of the bus into a sea of slime. The rain trickled down our necks and the few people that were about were about were more interested in their own predicament than in ours. We could not find anyone who spoke English or could read the Roman version of the name of our hotel. At last, although we felt sure that it must be just around the corner, we gave up the attempt to be self-sufficient and adventurous and took a taxi that happened to be standing near the bus park.

When the taxi drove us across the pitted, puddled forecourt it was to put us down in front of one of the most modern, luxurious — and expensive — hotels that we had stayed in since we arrived in Israel. One of the Israeli principles is that the best services should go to the perimeter. If there is a shortage of refrigerators then they ought to go to the remote villages and not to the central towns. It is in the desert and the difficult country places that any extra comfort or luxury that can be afforded should make its contribution. The cities will get more than their fair share anyway, the state's duty is to see that those who undertake the arduous tasks of development on the frontiers of its civilisation have the best services and equipment that can be provided for them. It seemed a refreshing and sensible idea, and directly contrary to our own where to be on the fringes is to have whatever life-blood there is gradually withdrawn. So, in the outpost that was Beersheba, we stepped thankfully out of the pouring rain into the spacious, welcoming entrance hall of our hotel.

Only one thing was wrong. The hotel was very new and it had been built, among other things, to withstand high temperatures. It was completely air-conditioned throughout. Now, quite suddenly, by a freak storm, Beersheba was shivering in an unaccustomed cold, and no one knew exactly how to operate the mechanism which would turn a cooling machine into a heating one. It could be done, but at the moment when we arrived the secret had not yet been found. The manager gave us our room number and the key, and explained that he would send a man along with us to regulate the heating. We were preceded along the carpeted corridor by a robust workman with

PETROL STATION SIGN

his bag of tools, who climbed up on to the desk and tinkered once or twice with the air-conditioning plant in a knowledgeable way. Then he smiled, assured us that all was well and left. With a sigh of satisfaction we inspected the private bathroom, bounced on the beds and prepared to relax. My husband went back to the desk to make some enquiries about our arrangements next day, and I sank into the comfort of a hot bath. Ten minutes later I emerged to find the air-conditioning gone mad and pumping great gouts of icy water out all over the room!

We were moved, with many apologies, to another bedroom, but the heat did not appear there either and in the end, like the other guests, we were driven into the dining-room-cum-bar which happened to be the only room equipped with an old-fashioned wall electric fire.

It was the off season for Beersheba as a tourist centre. It is the jumping-off point for the Negev, the new town of Arad, Sodom on the Dead Sea, the archaeological diggings at Massada, and the road route to Eilat, and it has still a romantic Bedouin market. Sooner or later most visitors to Israel pass through it. Now, however, there were only three other people, stranded by the rain which had prevented their tour going through, and the bulk of the custom was composed of groups of immensely tough men, the frontiersmen of the desert, engaged on all kinds of building and engineering and agricultural works, who came in for meals bringing with them the breath of another, more primitive and more urgent, world.

Certainly they could not have differed more from our other companions with whom we joined forces round the tiny fire. The husband and wife were from Michigan, U.S.A., of German-Jewish origin, on a three months tour of Israel. They had saved for years for this trip, not so much as a pilgrimage but because they felt it to be the done thing. The husband had served in the First World War, Kaiserlich und Königlich Infantry Regiment No. 90, he told us proudly and was surprised because my husband knew something of the reputation of the K. und K. Both this man's parents had died in concentration camps, but he and his wife had lived now very many years in America, prosperous small business people who had never till this venture moved far from the town where they had made their home. The trip was proving a terrible

BEERSHEBA PIONEERS

disappointment, and this Beersheba rain was the last straw. They felt personally affronted by it. Silly and selfish, they saw nothing at all of the miracle that was Israel but only how enormously it fell short, in their estimation, of their home town in the U.S.A.

The third member of the party was a man, a solitary, pathetic figure. He was an elderly South African, on a trip to Israel to visit his son who lived outside Tel Aviv, and he had decided to make the tour to Eilat because so many people had told him he ought to go there. In the long, wet evening he told us a lot about his children. He was a widower, an importer of delicacies into South Africa, with a daughter in London whom he visited every alternate year and this son in Tel Aviv. He loved the son, and was totally without understanding of him. He described to us how one day, when he was already married and doing well in the business, the son had told him that he was thinking of leaving South Africa and emigrating to Israel. Did we, he asked, understand why he should have wanted to do this? Could not South Africa give him everything in the way of a full life that a young man would want? We did understand, we had seen enough by now of the call to young Jews of a homeland of their own to find it easy to comprehend the pull of such an idea. Perhaps particularly in South Africa, where the luxurious affluence of his privileged life may well have roused mixed feelings in one who felt himself inwardly drawn towards minorities who were oppressed. But for his father, even after several visits to Israel, it was a continuing mystery. He described how the young man had pulled up all his roots, abandoned the inducements of property inherent in his father's business and taken off with his wife for the great adventure. It was on his daughter-in-law that the father had pinned his hopes.

'She could do nothing,' he said to us. 'She'd always had servants in the house, the best of everything. She enjoyed herself. I couldn't see her settling down to do her own work, living rough, cooking and cleaning and having no time for sports and entertainments. I felt sure she'd bring him back in a year or two. Let him try, I thought, he'll soon find out.'

But she had not brought him back. When the invitation came to visit them the next year he had been astonished and very perplexed to find that his son was deeply happy and his daughter-in-law had made herself into an efficient housekeeper and was going to present him with a grandson on the strength of it. That was some years ago.

The son was doing well and getting on, they had moved into a new flat, and every other year they asked him for a long visit; but he remained profoundly lonely and sad for he could still not understand what it was that had made his son leave the country of his birth, with all its riches, for this one. The pleasure he had once taken in building up the business was gone, because there was no longer anyone left to inherit it, and his grandson spoke Hebrew and was a stranger to him. We could not help contrasting him, even while we tried too late to add our attempts at explanation, with Dan's father, who had said in his middle age to his son: 'This is what I have always dreamed about, now that the opportunity has come shall we do it together?'

The next morning we were collected early by the agricultural instructor for this area. He was a big, burly man who had been a German, born in Poland, which he had left at the age of eighteen. One of five brothers, they had not been prepared to bear the insults in the years of open persecution which gradually worsened after 1933. When they were accosted in the streets they answered back. One day, as was inevitable, they got into a fight and beat up two young Nazis. That night a crowd arrived and destroyed half their house, but our guide had left already—over the border to Czechoslovakia where he spent two years. Then he managed to get to Palestine. Later three brothers joined him here, one remaining behind with the parents. As times got worse this brother was taken off and spent six months in Dachau until, in 1938-39, some sort of a trade with Eichmann got him out of the camp to Sweden where he settled. Now only the parents were left. With a smile at us which was half apologetic, half triumphant, our guide said:

'I found a British Officer here, in Palestine as it was then, who would give me an immigration permit for them for £50. We brought them out. They landed in Palestine on September 1st 1939, the day the papers announced that Poland had been invaded.'

The rain, after a night of deluge, had stopped and the sky was washed and clean over the enormous expanse of flat land. Here, for the first time, Israel looked immense, stretching away from horizon to horizon, the sweep of the land barely broken by the rows of young crops and the scattered pinpoints of villages. Only the trees along the dead straight roads, planted they said at the express wish of Ben Gurion ('I must see trees in the desert,' he had said), made any attempt to reach for the sky; and every now and again a huge, prehistoric monster of a truck, filled with potash or other minerals, thundered up these same roads from Dimona and Sodom and the salt shores of the Dead Sea.

It is in the Negev that future physical development lies. Money, science and workers are all needed, and if that development is to be agricultural as well as industrial then the Jordan water is of vital importance. Israel is trying every approach to get the two million Jews who remain in Russia out of that country, though so far every attempt has been blocked. 'But where would you put them?' we said several times, gazing round at the highly cultivated northern plains. 'In the Negev,' was always the answer. 'They could revolutionise the Negev.'

The new town of Arad, which will be an industrial city for the Negev is rich in minerals, has a high pioneering priority. A family moving there is given a donum of land by government if they agree to build their own house on it within a year. Already a great deal of expert technical knowledge is going into the problems of the Negev; the difficulties of excessive salination of the soil, the use of dew farms, the kind of crops which will bind and transform the desert. If determination, skill and faith can make the Negev blossom, then the Israelis are certain that blossom it will.

There are no delinquents in the desert, we were told, life is too raw and too gripping; but there may well be delinquents on the frontiers of the great sands, in the towns which service the growing stream of technicians and workers. 'It is there that we need the boys from the kibbutzim,' said a Minister. 'An honest young kibbutznik in the tax office at Beersheba could make an immense contribution. 'It is in this sort of situation that the second generation could find their challenges.

The rain had left its havoc behind. The first village we came to was one of Moroccan farmers, and the moment the car stopped we were surrounded by them, some wrapped shivering from the cold in white burnous, all of them obviously agitated and wanting

NEGEV VILLAGE

advice. They had been flung into confusion by the unaccustomed storm, and now, like a crowd of children longed for grown-up re-assurance that all was not lost. It was the potato crop that had suffered. We climbed on to a tractor and drove out through the heavy earth to see the damage. The weight of falling water had dislodged the potatoes, and had swept many of them right out of their proper fields. They lay about, naked and exposed, at this moment healthy looking but ready in a short time to rot away. In one case the farmer has cross-ploughed his field in the wrong direction, so that the water had done the maximum damage, a neat, if unfortunate, object lesson.

At first sight there was nothing to distinguish the next village from any of the others. We drove off the highway which ran straight through the flat landscape on to a muddy, bumpy track, but when we turned down between the houses we came across a crowd of children leaping up and down with cries of excitement beside a large puddle. They were excited, our guide said, because puddles were an event in this part of the world and this was the first rain of the season. Then we saw that each small boy wore a tiny round cap perched, sometimes very precariously it seemed, on the back of his head. This was the kippur, worn by all religious males. On either side of their cheeful, grinning faces in front of their ears hung two ringlets, long corkscrews which looked as if they had just been released from

RELIGIOUS VILLAGE

forcible twining round a stick. As they leapt in and out and over the puddle these curls jiggled and tossed in the air confusing for a moment the issue of the sexes until one saw again, as they stopped to gaze at us, the mischievous, male faces which they enclosed.

In the milk shed, where the produce came in to be prepared for market, there was a man at work who courteously stopped to speak to my husband. It was a poor village, and a small one, compared to Kfar Hess or some of the older moshavim, and the shed was simple and without complex machinery. Presently a little mule cart drove up loaded with milk churns and sacks of grain on top of which two more ringleted boys crouched. The bearded father got down and walked over to the shed to deliver his milk. He too politely stayed to talk, while the boys alternately cuffed each other spiritedly or looked curiously at me. What did he want his sons to do? my husband asked the man to which he replied that he wanted them to be craftsmen, to have a trade. Was this true of most of the boys, or did they want to stay on the land with their fathers? No, he replied, many fathers wanted their sons to study, to go away to religious schools where they could learn. Learning was the most important thing for a religious family, that their sons should become scholars of the Talmud. It was for this that the parents had striven and sacrificed and they did not want their sons to follow them on to the land. The desired professions were to become a religious court judge, which only the best could do, or a rabbi, or a teacher, or a craftsman of some kind. For them the study of the sacred Books and the knowledge of the Law remained the highest ideals.

The elderly father smiled and excused himself and went back to his mule cart. He gee-ed up the mule and the little vehicle went lurching and bumping off with the boys swaying perilously on top of the sacks. As we watched them grow gradually smaller in the distance our guide said:

'Many of the men in this village have wedded a second time. While they were in labour camps their wives were experimented on and doctored in concentration camps. That is why you will see so many young children in

BOY ON CART

MULE CART a village where all the men look elderly.'

Here, in this one morning, it seemed possible to see a whole cross-section of the Israeli population, all juxtaposed to one another and yet all still distinct and separate elements. As we drove out of Beersheba, where the land was still unreclaimed, from time to time a black Bedouin tent would appear pegged down on to the sand as though both needed desperately to cling to each other. Already they were anachronisms hemmed in by the encroaching tide of scientific research, the tents no longer romantic but somehow a ragged nuisance in their continuing bid for freedom, the sand gradually receding as the faint haze of green crept south. 'It's the Bedouin who've made the desert, not the desert the Bedouin,' said our guide, with the faintest flicker of contempt. Well, their creation was being transmuted now, and so too was their roving, nomadic life constricted from month to month and year to year. Soon they would have to be settled, somewhere, somehow.

The Moroccan farmers had inherited the earth, even if at this moment they were not very sure what to do with it and some maybe had nostalgic thoughts for the suqs which they had left to come here, where rain meant extra cups of tea while business slackened and no need to engage in any struggle with unwearying nature. The road to independence is a harsh one and they had not yet cast off the moorings which tied them to paternal authority. 'My roof is leaking,' said one. 'You gave us the house, what are you going to do about it?' he implied. And he huddled like a sick bird inside his burnous, shivering with the unaccustomed cold and fixing a beseeching eye on the instructor. But in the next village the young farmers who awaited us had suffered the same disaster but looked on it with different eyes. Advice they wanted, yes; mistakes had been made, yes; but they were ready even now to rectify them. These young men had come in as children, brought in by the Youth Aliya to rescue them from persecution, and they had been trained by the youth movement and in a kibbutz. For them the roots were firm, the identity established, they had no other land, no other occupation than this. In the religious village however, the land was a

MOROCCAN FARMER

means to an end, a base from which their sons could go on to the study of the Law.

As we passed one of the similar small houses in the Moroccan village I admired a cactus in the garden. We asked about it to be told that the house was closed, the owner, of Belgian origin, had gone to Dahomey for the Foreign Office as an agricultural expert. At that moment his neighbour appeared on her doorstep, and after some conversation asked us in to have a cup of coffee with her. The house was tiny and primitive, when we were all three with her in the little living-room it was quite full. Her hands were rough and hard with heavy work, but her heart was gay and warm, and her conversation sparkling. She was Hungarian, speaking to us in German. She and her husband had lived in a town in the north until three years before when he had been asked to come down as agricultural instructor to this new village so nearly in the desert. So she had come with him and she did not regret it. This was part and parcel of the meaning of Israel, that having been given a new life by the land they should in turn give it back to the land and through the land to others. She might miss the amenities of life in a town, the music and the contacts, the space and privacy of gracious living, but here she was joined to the life stream of a steady, continuing creative purpose and, for the time being, that was enough.

It was curious that having begun with a Hungarian, walking softly, taking care, our visit should end also with a Hungarian, walking proudly, living free.

Epilogue

So, I have written a book after all.

No one can capture a country between the pages of a book. I have not tried to do so. I have taken the aspects of Israel that interested us most and through them have attempted to recreate something of the flavour that a short experience of Israel held for two visitors.

If you now feel that you would like to see this country for yourself I shall be well satisfied.

SYRIA

LEBANON

Dan

Ayelet Hashahar

SEA
OF
GALILEE

R. JORDAN

Safad

Nazareth

GALILEE

Kfar Hess

Haifa

Ramat
Hadassah

Kfar Vitkin

Tel Aviv

ISRAEL

MEDITERRA